Scary Faith is pure gold! Tim does a masterful job pulling us from our safe and predictable lives and into our God-given destiny. I can only imagine what the Church would look like if everyone embraced the principles uncovered in these pages. Chock-full of powerful truths brought to life by Scripture and Tim's personal journey, this book will inspire and challenge you to step into a greater life.

Dr. Don Wilson
Founding Pastor of Christ's Church of the Valley
President of Accelerate Group
Phoenix, Arizona

In his book *Scary Faith*, Tim Moore opens the door for us in detail about stepping out in faith and how it can impact our lives in a significant way. We learn about stepping out in faith from biblical examples, popular movies, and his real-life experiences. This book is a must-read to help us better understand why we must trust in God. Thanks, Tim, for stretching our faith, but more importantly pointing to where we need to start!

Doug Crozier
CEO of The Solomon Foundation
Denver, Colorado

The concept of an easy faith or an inexpensive faith (one that won't cost us much) is completely foreign to Scripture. Walking by faith doesn't mean we won't be scared. In fact, it most likely means we will be terrified from time to time. Using the life of one of the Bible's most colorful characters, Tim carefully makes the case that scary faith isn't the exception. Rather, it's the extraordinary way of living God expects from all His children.

> **Barry L. Cameron**
> Senior Pastor of Crossroads and Author of *The ABC's of Financial Freedom, Contagious Generosity, & The Road to Financial Freedom*
> Grand Prairie, TX

WARNING: Don't pick up this book if you want a safe or easy life. These pages are not melatonin to help you sleep better in the boat. They're mega-jolts of caffeine and courage to help you step out of it. Out of the boat of paralysis, fear, and apathy, and onto an endless sea of possibilities and purpose. If you've ever felt that nagging ache that there's more to your life, more that's inside you, more to the dreams you've let die long ago and more to the future that until now you've been dreading, this book is for you. Stripped of cliches and easy answers, Tim takes us by the hand and leads us on a journey filled with vulnerability, fascinating insights from both Scripture and science, and into practical and powerful handles to overcome our fears and step into a life so beautiful only God could have dreamed it up.

> **Russ Moore**
> Executive Pastor at X Church and
> Author of *Hope for the Wilderness*
> Columbus, Ohio

As a pastor who planted a church with no training or financial backing, I can attest to the chilling aspects of faith. Conferences and mentors are sometimes helpful, but nothing compares to the fresh insight of someone who's walking through it now.

That's what Scary Faith does. It walks us through the journey with an assurance of hope and a call to action. I wish this book had been written before I started out. But I am thankful to be armed with it now as we face the next wave.

> **Matt Wilson**
> Lead Pastor of Ekklesia Christian Church
> Conway, SC

Tim's book is both challenging and uplifting. His real experiences, along with his humor and masterful storytelling skills, combine beautifully with his study of God and His Word to make an impressive, inspirational read. We are called to live out our faith, especially when it's scary, and Tim's book gives us the courage to do so.

Kristen Terrette
Author and Women's Ministry Leader
Woodstock, Georgia

Risk is a loaded word. Most of us avoid it and as a result lose the opportunity to experience something special or unique. Tim dares each of us to look inside ourselves and to God to discover what incredible future awaits us when we step out in faith. We all need to be pushed outside of our safe spaces and Tim does that in this book.

Keith Minier
Lead Pastor of Grace Fellowship
Pickerington, Ohio

I've had the privilege of watching Tim's journey firsthand. This book comes from his personal experience. One thing I've learned in life is that anytime you see success, there is always a price that was paid for it. Scary Faith is a place most never walk, but it's where miracles happen. Tim knows what's on the other side of

Scary Faith. This book shares the struggles and the victories of his journey and will infuse you with faith to take yours!

Konan Stephens
Lead Pastor of C3 Church and Founder of Venture Multiplication Network
Canal Winchester, Ohio

In my counseling work I regularly hear the words, "I'm stuck and I don't know what to do!" It's a statement fueled by frustration but often based in fear. In *Scary Faith*, Tim provides a tremendous guide to overcoming the fear that holds many people back from realizing their dreams. This book is practical, Biblical, and entertaining. You will not only be encouraged but your life can be changed for the better by reading *Scary Faith*.

Dr. Wes Beavis, Psy.D.
Clinical Psychologist and Author of *Let's Talk About Ministry Burnout*
Newport Beach, California

SCARY FAITH

Overcome Fear and Step into
the Life You Never Imagined

TIM MOORE

Cover Art by Tucker Johnson

Foreword by Tim Liston

Photography by Christi Witt

Graphic Layout Design by Hannah Kelly

Published in Columbus, Ohio by Tim Moore

ISBN (Hardcover): 979-8-9857951-1-0

ISBN (eBook): 979-8-9857951-2-7

ISBN (Audiobook): 979-8-9857951-3-4

Library of Congress Control Number: 2022903112

ISBN (Paperback): 979-8-9857951-0-3

Dedicated to my wife, Lorelei.
Without your love and support, this book does not exist.
This is our story.

CONTENTS

FOREWORD

If you want to follow Jesus, you've got to get out of the boat. If you want to see God do more in your life than what you're thinking or planning, then you *must* get out of the boat. If you want to make an impact beyond what you could ever imagine: Get. Out. Of. The. Boat! And your boat can be anything — a new career at forty, a dream to start a non-profit, or, like so many of us, making a scary financial decision or move.

It has been a joy to watch Tim's journey of faith over these past few years. I feel like I've been on the phone with him while he has one foot on the deck of the boat and the other on the surface of the water. Over and over, I've watched his courage to lead with that rare combination of boldness, audacity, and wisdom. And I've also watched God come through for him in big ways.

And yet... the big steps of faith in this season of his life and ministry are still "in process." I love that. In my mind, it gives him a unique voice that sets him apart from others. It is from this raw, special vantage point that he gives us an extremely candid, inspiring, and practical view of faith.

I've read a lot of books where the author is on the other side of the test. They got out of the boat, God did a miracle and now, from the comfort of the shoreline, they point out to the water and tell us what an awesome experience it was. And it's helpful. But Tim gives us a perspective that is far different and much needed. This is a guy standing in the middle of the lake. He's putting his full weight on the surface of the water, with the outcome "yet to be determined." Of course, those of us who follow Christ know the outcome. Or do we? If we know, why are some of us still in the boat?

This book is the missing piece for those who are thinking about stepping out in faith. It shows us someone who is still in the battle like we are. He's not on the distant shore cheering for us. He's next to us, shaking off his own doubts, watching both miracles and waves, and calling out the faith in himself and in us.

I know his words will encourage you to take steps of faith, even if that means your next step is over the side of the boat and onto the water.

Tim Liston
Senior Pastor of New Hope Church
Houston, TX

PROLOGUE

I'M NOT SURE IF this is going to work.

Have you ever said those words to yourself as you dipped your toes into unfamiliar waters? I must have said those words to myself a hundred times over the past few years. I have felt my faith swell with breakthroughs and dissipate with setbacks.

I'm pretty sure my anxiety would make a great emotional sphygmomanometer (the blood pressure cuff thingy). When it's up, so is my blood pressure. I know the thrill of attempting something so bold and risky that if it doesn't work, well, my life's work is over. I have found it hard to breathe at times, experienced panic attacks, and even felt like I was having a nervous breakdown — all because I was responding to God's call on my life.

Sound exciting?

Maybe terrifying?

It's both. And I'm convinced that's what a life of faith really looks like.

If you can't recall the last time you felt this way, perhaps it's time to push from the safety of the harbor out into open waters where anything can happen. Could it be your fear of failure is keeping you from the kind of life you could, or perhaps should, be living?

I'm convinced many of us are living a life that is safe, predictable, and boring.

We know exactly what is going to happen each day — not much.

Does this sound familiar? We drop the kids off at school, put in our time at the office, do the evening routine of dinner and homework, tuck our kids in bed, and watch TV until we can't hold our eyes open any longer. Then, we get up and do it again. Round and round we go with the same predictable life until we no longer have any more trips to make around the sun.

Let's face it. The older you get, the more attractive that sounds. We just want to hold a steady job, pay the bills, enjoy a few luxuries, and hopefully retire to Florida to escape the snow. That is unless you live in Florida. In that case, I'm not sure where you go.

It is so tempting to embrace this kind of life. I'm just not sure that's what God intended this life to be. And I'm not sure it's fulfilling us. In fact, it could be dragging us silently to a very slow, boring death.

I'm not saying I want my life to be written in history books and taught to future generations. I'm not sure my story is that exciting; not to mention that sounds a bit narcissistic. But I do want my life to count for something. I want to think that because I existed, our world, or at least someone's world, got better. Don't you?

When I think about some of the people who have graced the pages of history books or re-written history with their exceptional story, I can't help but think about names written in Hebrews Chapter 11 of the New Testament. For Christians, this chapter is the 'who's who' of history-makers. These Hall of Famers have a story worth telling our three-year-olds in Sunday School. You can always tell how important someone's story is by what we teach our kids in church.

Noah.

He's beloved for saving all the animals! Every kid needs a coloring page of an ark with animals walking up the long plank.

Joshua.

He's our brave warrior. I remember walking around in a circle to music before we "all fall down" (to the floor) like the walls of Jericho. Good times.

David.

Well, he's the legend. How many people are remembered for slinging a stone at a giant and then decapitating him? Of course, we never read that part of the story to our toddlers.

While I don't think I want to be known for killing someone and cutting their head off, in a small way I would love to know my story matters. That when my life is over, I wouldn't be so forgettable. My guess is that you do as well.

What I'm trying to say is, we all want to have had a story like Noah, Joshua, or David, but rarely do we want to walk in their shoes. Would you like to be ridiculed for decades while building some crazy-looking structure that probably resembles a tree house more than a boat? I find it hard to believe Noah's wife didn't get mad whenever he went to the backyard to work on his "God-project" while leaving half of her fix-it list undone. Not that I'm saying this from personal experience.

And what about Joshua? Would you want to lead a bunch of college-age frat boys with no real-world fighting experience into battle against impossible odds and a fortified city? It sounds like the makings for a Hollywood blockbuster, but for Joshua it had to be terrifying. Just imagine his entire army complaining because he's making them play Ring-Around-The-Rosie until they all fall dead.

Then there's David. He was one of the greatest kings Israel ever had. He was wealthy, adored by many, and wrote love songs better than John Legend. But very few of us would ever like to stare down a lion in the open country or go toe-to-toe with a 500-pound warrior who was dead set on feeding our flesh to the vultures.

This is the part of their stories that is often overlooked. We remember their exploits, but rarely do we consider what it was like to walk in their shoes. I find it is easy to get jealous of other people's accomplishments without considering what they had to go through to achieve them. I love the idea of being the victor, but I'm not sure I like the thought of fighting for my life.

My point is this, doing something great for God always comes with great adversity. Doing something significant with your life will probably be more difficult than you've ever imagined. All I know is I don't want to get to the end of my life and think, "I wish I had tried…" When I consider which emotion is worse, the fear of failing or the regret for not trying, I always default to regret. The thought that my purpose was passing me by and I didn't do anything to grab it by the tail seems to me the greatest tragedy of all.

Is it scary? Unbelievably.

Will it be worth it? I'll let you know at the end.

Will it make a difference? Ask someone at my funeral.

I honestly never thought I would write a book about faith. Experts write books. People who have accomplished great things write books to tell you how they did it. People who built Fortune 500 companies or successfully led organizations to greatness have a secret to share with the rest of us. I get that. You should buy their books. After all, who wants to read a book written by someone who may or may not succeed? It reassures our faith when we know how the story ends. In fact, the entire Christian faith rests on the end of a story where Jesus walks out of a tomb... alive again.

But what is often overlooked is the *middle* of these stories. We seldom get insight into what our heroes of faith were experiencing while waiting for a miracle. We rarely get to feel what Jesus' disciples felt in those hours they believed their leader was gone forever. We almost never get to hear from someone who is working out his faith while he is wrestling with fear.

So, I thought, why not write a book to tell my journey with faith while I'm *in the middle of it.* When it comes to faith, I'm not an expert — I'm a practitioner. I'm writing this book while living out the scariest moments of my life. This isn't some Hardy Boys mystery where I can pick the ending. As I write these words, I don't know how my story will end.

Perhaps writing this book is me living by faith while living in the uncertainty of tomorrow. I hope my story will inspire you to step out of the boat or, at the very least, give you a roadmap of what *not* to do. Either way, it's going to be real. It's going to be honest. And it's going to meet you in the middle of *your* story.

My prayer for you while reading this book is that you will be prompted to attempt something so significant it might fail. I pray God would revive a dream or notion you left behind because it was just too scary. Whether you are a stay-at-home mom, an entrepreneur, pastor, or college student, all of us have God-given dreams yet to be fulfilled.

The real question is whether you will settle in the plains of comfort or adventure by faith into your destiny.

I believe only in those moments will you find the kind of life God intends for you to live.

PROLOGUE

Only in that place will you experience what it means to live by faith.

1

TIDAL WAVES

"To reach a port we must set sail. Sail, not tie at anchor. Sail, not drift."
~ Franklin D. Roosevelt

EVER SINCE I WAS a kid, I've had a weird obsession with tidal waves. In fact, I love any kind of grossly oversized waves. Earlier this year, I visited Hawaii for the first time. It was even more beautiful than depicted in the movies. One particular day at the beach, the lifeguards put stakes with red flags in the sand which apparently means the ocean is angry. The ocean didn't look angry to me; it looked inviting. The waves were calling my name like a charm swaying back and forth in the hands of a hypnotist. My wife pleaded with me not to go into the water. But it was too late. I was under its spell.

Like a zombie, I waded out to chest-deep water, fighting the angry monster's grip on my feet. As I approached what I thought was an eight or nine-foot wave (only later to find out it was only about a six-foot wave), I snapped out of my hypnotic state. I did not want to die that day. I waved a white flag and turned in shame toward dry ground.

Let me be clear. I'm obsessed with huge waves, even though I have no interest whatsoever in riding any of them. I've never even been on a surfboard. I'm just strangely drawn to the power of the ocean and its ungodly, over-sized waves. It's on my bucket list to witness Oahu's massive winter waves that can sometimes reach upwards of fifty feet tall. It will be like taking a nine-year-old kid to Disney World.

I think it all started during my impressionable, adolescent years when I watched an old movie called *The Poseidon Adventure*. The movie, based on the fictional novel *The Poseidon Adventure* by Paul Gallico, tells the story of a transatlantic ocean liner being flipped upside down by a ninety-foot wall of water on New Year's Eve.

I know what you are thinking: "I need to watch this movie!" Before you waste 117 minutes of your precious life on this 1972 classic, might I suggest watching some of the newer remakes with better special effects. For whatever reason, this movie started my childhood obsession and fear of tidal waves.

Luckily, I lived in Ohio.

My family rarely took vacations to the beach when I was growing up. So, when we finally did, I was filled with a sense of excitement and trepidation. After all, that's where tidal waves happen.

We made the ten-hour road trip from Ohio to Rehoboth Beach, Delaware. Road trips were always interesting with three kids jammed into the backseat. For a little perspective, this was before smartphones, portable DVD players or even Gameboy existed. I know... some of you can't fathom how we survived that long in the car without those necessities. To be honest, I can't either. We passed most of the time reading books, playing the license plate game, and fighting for every square inch of leg room.

Wars sometimes erupted when someone's knee crossed the Intercontinental Divide into your airspace. Good times.

Our first morning there, we grabbed our towels, boogie boards, and sand tools and ran to the beach.

"First one to the beach wins," one of us would yell.

My siblings and I turned everything into a competition. I still have fond memories of playing *paddle ball* in the hot sun. Paddle Ball was a game we constructed out of two wooden paddles and a little blue rubber bouncy ball. We would dig the outline of a court in the sand with our heels and then play our own version of beach tennis until there was a champion. My dad even got into the action, so it became a tournament. Whether on sea or dry ground, everything became a competition. Even playing in the waves.

We also used to play a game where we stood waist deep in the ocean as waves crashed right into us. The goal — stay upright. The loser was the first one knocked off their feet. What I discovered is no matter how much violence I could withstand, the clear-cut winner was always the ocean. Even relatively little breakers can have a way of making you feel small and powerless.

But nighttime is when everything changed for me. That is when my fear of the ocean came alive. I would lie awake in my bed every night with fearful thoughts flooding my mind. "What if the shore is scrolling back into the sea right now and no one is awake to see it? What if a massive wall of water is coming for us right now?"

Panic would set in as I pictured water ebbing away from the shore in the blackness of night. I was convinced every night at the beach would probably be my last. Thus, never were the words of this fateful bedtime prayer ever so true:

> "Now I lay me down to sleep; I pray the
> Lord my soul to keep. If I should die before
> I wake, I pray the Lord my soul to take."

By the way, parents, never pray that with your kids right before you shut off the lights.

Every night, tidal waves were the last thing on my mind as I drifted off to sleep. This might explain why I had so many nightmares while on vacation. I often dreamed of a rushing surge lifting my bed off the ground as the walls of our house started collapsing in on us. Sheer terror would fill the house with screams dissipating to underwater moans as we all succumbed to a watery grave. You can imagine my relief when I finally woke up and saw my bedroom floor was dry, even if the bed wasn't. I would run out to the family room and look out the windows toward the beach, and sure enough... everything was exactly where God left it.

Phew, another night survived.

Often in life we can live in fear of an unlikely tidal wave. It might not be a ninety-foot wall of water; it could be fear of losing your job. You might be afraid you will never find someone special and get married. Or you might have a fear your kids will be messed up because you did something wrong. Surely all of these things *could* happen to us. But it's also possible none of them will. You may end up getting promoted, meet someone special next month, and your kids might grow up to be responsible, competent parents of their own.

I'm not saying some of our fears are unfounded. The reason we are afraid of something is because it *actually* happened to someone at some point. My oldest daughter, Lauryn, is scared to death of sharks even though she has never encountered one in the wild. However, because she watched a movie of a teenage surfer from Hawaii whose arm was bitten off by a shark, it's nearly impossible to get her into the ocean. My fear of tidal waves is real because there have been devastating tidal waves, even if I've never witnessed one.

If we aren't careful, fear can paralyze us and keep us from living the adventurous and fulfilling life God invites us to experience. Fear can reduce our lives to safe, predictable routines that inspire no one — not even ourselves. I'm just not sure *safe* is the best descriptor for a Jesus-follower. In fact, when you read the Bible, you will discover everyone who was used by God in powerful ways had to face some real fears and take a step into the unknown.

Meet Peter.

Not my older brother Peter.

Not Peter Parker.

We'll just call him Peter. He doesn't really have a last name. He's just Peter from the Bible. Well, actually his parents named him Simon, but Jesus thought he acted more like a Peter. So, Simon is really Peter, clear? I'm just going to refer to him as Peter because it's easier that way.

We are first introduced to Peter in Luke's Gospel as Jesus was beginning his ministry. In Luke 5, Jesus is already attracting a crowd with his preaching on the shore of the Sea of Galilee. This was the area where Jesus spent most of his time. As the crowd grew, Jesus looked for a way to facilitate the multitude of people. He saw two empty boats on the shore, walked over and hopped into one of them. You can probably guess whose boat it was. Yep, it was Peter's boat. Jesus asked if Peter would push out from the water's edge so he could continue his sermon. This was a common practice in those days. Teachers would use the surface of the water to amplify their voice for large gatherings.

Peter was nice enough to oblige and pushed the boat out from the shore so Jesus could finish the last two points of his sermon. As soon as Jesus wrapped up his sermon with a moving story that had people in tears, he turned to Peter and asked him to do something that made no sense.

> When he had finished speaking, he said to
> Simon, "Put out into deep water, and let
> down the nets for a catch."
>
> [Luke 5:4]

I'm sure this was the last thing Peter wanted to do at that moment. I can't imagine what it would be like to fish all night in ancient Galilee. They didn't just throw a line or two into the water, set the poles, and then prop their feet up on the edge of the boat and crack open a cold one. In those days, they fished using nylon nets with weights tied around the edges. You would heave the weighted nets over the side of the boat and then pull them back into the boat like you're climbing a rope in gym class. Can you imagine doing that three or four hundred times every night? Surely there would be no reason to keep your Planet Fitness membership. Not to mention they had been up all night doing this while Jesus was most likely sleeping.

Why was this Rabbi asking a professional fisherman to go fishing in the daylight hours? Every successful fisherman knew the best time to fish was at night. I learned this simple lesson the first time I went fishing with my older brother, Peter, who also loved to fish. Perhaps all Peters like to fish. Who knows?

I was about ten years old when he took me to a small fishing hole in rural Ohio. We went early in the morning because the fish come to the surface to eat when the temperature is cooler. I distinctly remember sitting on the shore for hours staring at a red and white bobber that never bobbed. Not once. I didn't even get a single nibble on my line. Later, I would learn how much you need the feedback of a fish pecking at your bait every so often to keep you hooked, even if they never do.

That day, the fish must have eaten everything but our worms. Finally, with the relentless midday sun beating down on our necks, we lost all hope of catching any fish. It was hot, miserable, and intensely boring. That one trip pretty much cut short my professional fishing career. I haven't been on speaking terms with fishing since that day.

So, it makes sense that Peter (the one from ancient Galilee) and his brother went fishing during the night. I imagine Peter was exhausted, worn out, and ready for his bed. Based on his response to Jesus, you can assume he had no desire to charter a fishing excursion with this Rabbi.

> Simon answered, "Master, we've worked hard
> all night and haven't caught anything. But
> because you say so, I will let down the nets."
>
> [Luke 5:5]

There are two significant things that happen in this moment.

First, Peter makes sure to state his objection up front. I have to admit, I would have done this too. I'm pretty sassy and, like Peter, would have thrown in an unnecessary comment. This was Peter's way of telling Jesus, "I told you so," before they catch a whole lot of *nothing* again.

Second, Peter responds in obedience to this Rabbi. Even though Peter makes sure Jesus knows how improbable his request is, he then proceeds to do it anyway. Although we come to find out Peter tends to talk back to Jesus (Matt 16:22, John 13:8, Luke 22:31-32), he is also a person of action.

What we find in this moment is an example of *faith*. Peter's experience fishing the night before leads him to believe they won't catch any fish. But his respect and trust for this Rabbi propels him to act without knowing for sure what will happen. Though the word faith isn't used in this passage, the context of faith is implied.

In my opinion, the word "faith" in our English language has become benign and ambiguous. It carries nearly as many references as the word "love" does. People love their spouse, love their car, and love a good pizza. And yes, I personally love all of these.

The Ancient Greeks used at least seven different forms for the context of love: Eros (romantic), Phila (friendship), Ludus (playful), Storge (familial), Pragma (committed), Philautia (self-love), and Agape (unconditional). Perhaps this is why God chose Hebrew and Greek as the primary languages for recording His revelation to humanity through the Scriptures. Those languages do a much better job dealing with nuance of tense and meaning than English does. Not to mention a better way to describe the breadth of God's love toward us more accurately.

In our Western culture, the term *faith* carries many different meanings. Faith can represent a belief in the existence of God, a powerful form of trust, a necessary ingredient to receive a miracle, a way to combat someone with a negative attitude (have a little faith), or a means of encouraging someone when they want to quit on life (keep the faith). No wonder the very concept of faith used in the Bible has lost much of its meaning in our Western linguistic reference.

As I talk about faith in this book, I'm primarily speaking of an *active* faith and not just a religious belief or encouragement for someone going through a rough patch. I would contend that part of the problem with Western Christianity is the willingness to adopt faith as a passive term rather than what we discover while reading through the pages of Scripture.

While I agree that it takes a basic form of faith to believe in God's existence, I also believe it takes a different type of faith to orient your life around Jesus' commands. Jesus almost always invited people to *follow* Him, not just believe in Him. Faith should create movement in our lives. Faith is not just a framework for our theology, it's a pair of shoes for our feet. Although the word faith is a noun, it should really be treated more like a verb.

The kind of faith Peter demonstrates is an *active* faith. Although it probably made no sense, Peter still pushed out into the deep to fish in the hot midday sun. An active faith responds to the call of God, even if it seems to make no sense. This is the only real version of faith I see demonstrated by Jesus' followers in the New Testament.

FAITH IS NOT JUST A *FRAMEWORK* FOR OUR THEOLOGY, IT'S A PAIR OF *SHOES* FOR OUR FEET.

Today, there are many Christians who have fooled themselves into adopting a belief system in an all-powerful God as long as they don't have to act upon that belief. Yet, James, the half-brother of Jesus, tells us, "Faith by itself, if it is not accompanied by action, is dead." (James 2:17). In other words, what we believe *must line up* with how we live. Period.

Peter does what Jesus asks him to do, even if under objection. At some point in your journey of faith, you should have moments when you respond to what God is asking you to do, even if it makes no sense at the time. These are the moments you say "yes" to Jesus, even if under objection.

I made the life-changing decision when I was seventeen years old to follow Jesus. That meant whatever Jesus asked me to do, I would do it, no questions asked. Okay, that is not true. I'm going to ask a lot of questions and might even let Jesus know how foolish it seems. But, if Jesus asks me to do something, even if it seems pointless, I'm in.

Peter pushed out into the deep, which is a fancy way of saying he rowed the boat out to the middle of the lake. I wonder if he rolled his eyes or even sighed out loud a couple times just to make sure Jesus knew how dumb this idea really was. I know I would have certainly done that. When he finally reaches deep enough water, Peter heaves the net over the side of the boat with a grunt and what happened next humbled him.

> When they had done so, they caught such a large number of fish that their nets began to break.
>
> [Luke 5:6]

Where did all these fish come from?

Where were they when I was out here last night?

And how did this Rabbi know the fish would be here now?

I wonder how many thoughts raced through Peter's mind as his cheeks turned rosy with embarrassment. In fact, he caught so many fish his nets started to break, and he had to call to his fishing partners in the other boat to come help.

Peter can't even look Jesus in the eye after this moment. All he could do was fall to his knees in that wooden boat and apologize for questioning Him. Peter felt so guilty for his bad attitude and doubting spirit that he even asked Jesus to go away from him. Although, I'm not sure what Peter expected Jesus to do in the middle of the lake, just walk away... (where? on the water!) Silly Peter, that's impossible.

What follows this exchange is another one of those faith moments.

> Then Jesus said to Simon, "Don't be
> afraid; from now on you will fish for people."
> [Luke 5:10b]

Matthew's Gospel account gives us the definitive invitation Jesus gave.

"Come follow me."

[Matthew 4:19]

Here again was a test of Peter's faith. You have to remember at this moment Peter didn't know Jesus would end up being the Savior of the world. It's possible Peter heard the rumors that were already circulating about this Rabbi. But he surely didn't think Jesus was straight out of heaven. And now, with their biggest catch to date, Jesus simply asks Peter to walk away from it all!

Who would do that?

I don't think we can overlook the enormity of what Jesus asked Peter and his fishing partners to do. Fishing was how they fed their families. Fishing was their trade. Fishing was their life. And in one brief, miraculous moment Peter is asked to give it all up to follow a Rabbi?

I wonder if Peter even took a moment to consider the implications of this decision. Can you imagine the questions that would ping-pong through his mind?

Follow you where?

How will I feed my family?

What will my wife say when she hears what I just did?

In what seems like a rash decision that makes no sense at all... Peter leaves it all behind and follows Jesus.

Irresponsible?

Perhaps.

Everything about this decision defies logic. Who shuts down their business the moment they have their best quarter? Who walks away from valuable assets and cash in the bank to a penniless invitation?

Peter.

The world would say he was crazy. His wife probably made him sleep on the couch when he went home to pack his bags. His parents had to be worried. It simply doesn't add up. What would cause someone to walk away from his business goals, guaranteed salary with benefits, and job security?

Faith.

So, let me drop a secret on you right in the first chapter. Ready?

Peter wasn't the only one called to this kind of life. *You and I are also called to it.* The echo of Jesus' invitation still reverberates thousands of years later. It's an invitation to something new and uncertain, something exciting and yet scary.

But let's not confuse who gave the invitation. Peter didn't invite Jesus into his boat or, should we say, his life. It was the other way around. Jesus invited Peter to leave his old life for a better one. Jesus was upgrading Peter's calling to fishing for men. The life Jesus called Peter to was far greater than the one he was already living.

The same is true for you and me. In fact, everyone who chooses to follow Jesus is invited to leave behind their safe and predictable life for an adventurous life of faith. If you have any question what this book is about, this is it! It's about leaving behind safety and comfort to step into the life you *never* imagined. Yes, it will be scary to leave behind what you know. But it's worth it. It's an upgrade. It's a life filled with miracles, meaning, purpose, and, best of all, joy!

But I must warn you. Living by faith will cause you to do some things that just don't make sense on paper. Following Jesus will sometimes lead you in a direction with no destination in view. It might lead you to the edge of insanity and will surely have you second guessing yourself and God. A life of faith is exciting and, as this book will demonstrate, *it can be very scary*. But honestly, there's no other way to really live this life to its fullest. This is the life God calls us to live for Him. Anything less is second best.

Now, before you put this book down and call your boss to quit your job and list your house on Zillow so you can chase your dream to be a missionary in Africa, let's slow down a little. I'm not suggesting God wants you to walk away from your career or move to another city to become a pastor or missionary. But what I *am* saying is that Jesus is calling you to walk away from having *control* over those things.

In the same way that Peter had to learn to submit to Jesus when asked to push out into the deep, Jesus is going to ask you and me to do the same. That means surrendering to God your dreams for the future, your five or ten-year plan, and your goals of financial success in order to embrace His purpose for your life. Before you think this sounds like an unfair proposition, let me remind you that what Jesus offered Peter was so much greater than what he was leaving behind. What Peter received was worth infinitely more than his fishing business would ever give him. The same is true when we respond to Jesus' invitation to follow him into our unknown future.

You see, living by faith is like going to the beach. If a tidal wave doesn't hit, you'll probably have the time of your life.

TIDAL WAVES

I hope I never experience a tidal wave.

2

THE INVITATION

"Adventure is the invitation to common people to become uncommon."

~ *Warren Miller*

M Y WIFE IS OBSESSED with the beach. It's her favorite place in the world. It's also the only place we go on vacation. Almost every year we talk about options for other places to take our family. I always suggest going out West to see the desert, roam the mountains, and explore the National Parks. She always wants to go to a beach, sit in the surf, and bake in the sun. Over the years, we've learned what makes a marriage work — compromise. So, every year we go to the beach!

One of my favorite things to do at the beach is body surf. It's a skill my dad taught me when I was kid. He taught me to wade out to chest-deep water and scan the horizon for the biggest breaker you could find. He told me that you can't be in a rush. That it's all about finding the right wave.

Something inside of you begins to stir the moment you lock eyes with the perfect wave. If you are quiet enough, you can hear it taunting you, calling you out for an after-school fight. As it approaches, you turn your body toward the shore while never losing eye contact with your nemesis. Just as you feel the wave pulling you closer for a kiss, throw your body into a plank position and start pulling and kicking like it has halitosis. If you catch the wave just right, you will feel it lift you to the top. As the wave breaks, you'll be propelled, effortlessly gliding to the shallows.

That's if it works.

I'll never forget the moment I learned to respect the power of the ocean. Fresh off my body surfing instruction, I was catching three and four-foot breakers at Rehoboth Beach. I was getting bolder with each victorious ride. Surely I was up on the scorecard.

Unfortunately, I didn't realize it would only take one punch to end this duel.

I waded out to deeper water, diving through small breakers looking for a prizefight. Finally, I caught a monstrous wave. Or so I thought. I quickly realized it had caught me. Instead of gliding to the top, it rolled me over and picked me up like a WWE wrestler and DDT body-slammed me on the ground. The wave drove my back into the ocean floor and proceeded to toss me around underwater like a ragdoll. I washed up on shore with bloodied knees and sinuses filled with salt water.

Knockout.

The fight was over.

I've always been puzzled about how body surfing works. Well, not just body surfing, but water buoyancy in general. We all know if you put something heavy in water it sinks. If you jump in the deep end of the pool and do nothing, you'll sink to the bottom. Yet somehow massive cruise ships with thousands of people do not sink.

I do know there is an actual scientific explanation for water buoyancy.

If the upward force of the water's density is equal to the downward gravitational force of an object's displaced water weight, it will float.1 And yes, I had to look that up.

Apparently, this is why a small rock thrown into the sea will sink but a large ship won't. Even though the boat weighs more than the rock, it displaces more water than it weighs and therefore floats. I guess that's why you can stretch out your body in a Deadman's float position and not sink but if you try to stand up on water you'll drop every time. Honestly, I sink every time I try the Deadman's float too. Perhaps I'm just doing it wrong.

All I know is what happens in Matthew 14 doesn't seem to follow the laws of physics. But then again, a lot of things Jesus did broke universal laws. Jesus had just finished an all-day seminar with thousands of people in attendance. Near the end, He borrowed a boy's lunch of five loaves and two fish and miraculously multiplied it to feed five thousand men plus the women and children. Only Jesus can borrow someone's lunch and give it back with interest.

But that's not the miracle I'm talking about. Right after this happened, as the sun was about to set, Jesus told his disciples to get into a boat and make their way to the other side of the sea. It seems Jesus just needed some alone time. It's these moments that make me think Jesus might have been an introvert or could only take so much of His disciples.

By the way, if you ever get a chance to visit the Sea of Galilee, do it. It's beautiful! The sea is about eight miles wide and twelve miles long. Surrounded by the Galilean hills and mountains of the Golan Heights, the Sea of Galilee is about 700 feet below sea level. This unique setup often creates pop-up storms with intense winds. As the wind blows from the east, it shoots through the hills like a slingshot and creates gale-like winds on the sea.

Back to that evening. Jesus hiked up to an overlook on one of the mountains so He could pray. He had a bird's-eye view of the disciples' sunset cruise. The only problem was Jesus didn't check the weather app before He sent them off sailing. That evening a massive storm hit.

Threatened by the midnight gale, they spent hours rowing, but to no avail. If that wasn't bad enough, what they saw next in the dark, stormy night would be enough to cause anyone to pray or cuss or maybe do both. Here's how Matthew recorded this moment.

> Shortly before dawn Jesus went out to them,
> walking on the lake. When the disciples saw
> him walking on the lake, they were terrified.
> "It's a ghost," they said, and cried out in fear.
>
> [Matthew 14:25-26]

Apparently, Jesus decided to join His disciples in the middle of the lake. Only He didn't have a boat. So, He went out to them, *walking on the lake. Say what?* Hold on. Can we even talk about this rationally? Did Matthew just say Jesus came toward them walking on the lake without skipping a beat? And he says it in such a matter-of-fact way. Perhaps if you were around Jesus quite a bit, nothing surprised you anymore.

Even then, how terrifying this must have been. First, they thought this blurry figure out on the water was a ghost. At this point, I would imagine the ghost coming toward them was scarier than the midnight storm. This sort of feels like that classic horror movie scene. You know the one. Stranded in a car in the middle of the woods, an old, rusty pickup truck slowly pulling up behind.

> Jesus, realizing they don't recognize Him,
> tried to calm them down. But Jesus

immediately said to them: "Take courage! It
is I. Don't be afraid."

[Matthew 14:27]

There is so much to unpack in this one verse that we are
going to come back to this one in Chapter Four. All we know is
Jesus' statement doesn't really clear things up with His disciples.
In other words, if you are watching *Scooby-Doo*, the ghost hasn't
taken off his mask yet. I think I just dated myself with that
reference. If you have no idea who *Scooby-Doo* is, ask your parents.

Peter still isn't convinced the ghost is Jesus. But you have
to appreciate Peter's boldness in what he barks back to the ghost.
One of the things I love about Peter is that he's the guy who always
has something to say and he always says it. Honestly, I can totally
identify with him.

"Lord, if it's you," Peter replied, "tell me to
come to you on the water."

[Matthew 14:28]

I can think of a million other ways to verify it was really
Jesus. Right? I mean we all have to answer those annoying security
questions whenever we create an account online. What was the

make of your first car? Where did you meet your spouse? What was your first pet's name? If I'm Peter, I think I would have asked, "Lord, if it is you, in what city did you turn water into wine?" That's an easy one... Cana. I'm sure you guessed it right, too.

But not Peter. He asked Jesus to prove himself by inviting Peter to do the impossible. What a brilliant and gutsy request. A ghost might have the power to float on water, but only God can give Peter the power to break God's laws. Peter has been around water his whole life. He knows this is not humanly possible.

I think sometimes we settle for asking God for *too* little. We look at scary moments and just want reassurance. God, is it going to be okay? Am I going to survive this storm? But Peter looked into the storm and said to Jesus, *if You are in this, invite me into it.* For all of Peter's many faults, this is something we should admire about him. He doesn't just want to see God perform a miracle. He wants to be part of it.

If you are thinking, *I wish I was brave like Peter*, then you should know something. This isn't bravery. We know this because later when Peter has a chance to be brave, he becomes a coward and abandons Jesus. This isn't bravery. This isn't courage. This, my friends, is faith.

Faith isn't just a feeling.

Faith isn't just a belief system.

Faith is responding to God's invitation to do the impossible. Faith is stepping into an uncertain future because you believe God is there waiting for you. Perhaps I should also give you a well-known description of faith from the Bible.

> Now faith is confidence in what we hope
> for and assurance about what we do not see.
>
> [Hebrews 11:1]

Simply put, faith is having enough confidence in what you are hoping God will do that you are willing to act on it. The two critical words we need to understand in this verse are *confidence* and *assurance*. Permit me a brief lesson in the original language.

FAITH ISN'T JUST A BELIEF SYSTEM.

The Greek word for confidence is *hupostasis* which means *a firm foundation*. It was a very common word used in those days to refer to any kind of structural foundation. Today, we might say it's the concrete footers for what we hope or believe will happen in the future.

The Greek word for assurance is *elegchos* which means either *proof* or *conviction*. It means having a strong conviction or enough evidence to believe something is true – even if you don't see it with your own eyes. Perhaps we can think about a jury that came to a unanimous conclusion based on the preponderance of evidence, even though they did not witness the crime.

My guess is Peter had never successfully walked on water before. Why do I think that? Because I have never seen anyone do it and, to be honest — I have tried it. I'm pretty sure most of us church kids who heard this story have tried running as fast as we can across the surface of a swimming pool. Don't look at me like that. I bet you've tried it too.

But Peter has a radical thought. If Jesus could walk on water, then perhaps *he* could as well. After all, this isn't the first time Peter had seen Jesus do the impossible. He'd just watched Jesus feed more than 5,000 men plus women and children with five barley loaves and two fish!

Is your faith more like Peter's or the rest of the disciples?

If I'm being honest, at times I live more like the hunkered-down disciples in the boat. I often choose cowering in the stern rather than stepping out of the boat. It's much easier to believe Jesus can do the impossible than it is to believe I can too.

How often I forget what Jesus said to his disciples just before he was arrested and crucified.

> "I tell you the truth, anyone who believes in me will do the *same* works I have done, and even *greater works*, because I am going to be with the Father."
>
> [John 14:12 NLT emphasis mine]

Imagine that! Honestly, it's hard to picture us doing greater things than what Jesus did while He was on earth. How is that even possible? Jesus raised the dead, healed the blind, cured skin diseases, and multiplied food! Some of you might just be trying to get through the work week without yelling at your co-workers or kids. Perhaps Jesus said his followers will do greater works because there would be *more* of them than Him and, therefore, they could accomplish a greater number of things. That I can understand, I guess. But how about the part where Jesus said, "anyone who believes in me will do the same works I have done." Have you ever considered this means *you* could do the same works Jesus did? Somehow, we have convinced ourselves that what Jesus said, "...with God all things are possible" (Matthew 19:27b), is true for Him but not for us.

If I had a magic wand, I would change something in our vernacular. I would separate the meaning of faith from the meaning of belief. I think our confusion in this area has led to a version of Christianity that is powerless, futile, and still hiding in the proverbial boat. If I had my way, we would stop calling it faith when someone *believes* that Jesus is God. Faith would be reserved for something more. Faith would describe what comes *after* we believe in Jesus.

The truth is, every time Jesus encountered faith, it was always in the context of someone asking him to do the impossible.

A father asked Jesus to heal his demon-possessed son.

The Centurion asked Jesus to heal his servant.

The lepers asked Jesus to cleanse them.

The two blind men asked Jesus for their sight.

All of these situations required action. All of these moments required faith. And perhaps our faith should be asking Jesus to do the impossible in our lives.

When was the last time you asked Jesus if you could get out of the boat? When was the last time you attempted something so scary that if God wasn't there you would sink? The reality is that many Christians won't even consider getting out of the boat.

They won't give a tithe to their church because their finances will be too tight.

They won't be public about their faith at school because they fear being made fun of.

They won't boldly pray with a friend who is sick because God may not heal her.

They won't go on a mission trip because they don't have the money or time.

Instead, many just crouch down in the bottom of the boat hoping to one day reach the other side of eternity. But is this the life that Jesus calls us to live? One that is dominated by fear or even worse, indifference? Is living inside the safety of the boat what Jesus meant when he said we will do *greater* works? It's hard to do anything significant for God if we're hiding in the hull.

Peter had the guts to *ask* Jesus if it would be possible for him to walk on water. It's one thing for Jesus, the Son of God, to pull it off; it's quite another for one of us to do it.

What's Jesus' response to this brave request?

"Come," he said.

[Matthew 14:29a]

One word.

I wonder if He said it in a loving or taunting type of voice. "Come on Peter... let's see what kind of faith you really have." Or maybe it was just a soft reply of confidence. We don't know. Matthew doesn't give us the inflection or tone, perhaps because he was hiding in the stern and couldn't see Peter's reaction. All we know is with a single word Jesus invited Peter into the realm of the impossible.

One word.

One step.

You see, Jesus invites us to experience life out on the open sea with Him. Rarely does He give us anything beyond *come*. He didn't give Peter any instructions for walking on water. All Jesus gave Peter was an invitation. And I'm convinced Jesus wants to extend to us the same simple invitation into a life of faith with Him.

I never knew how many times I would have to get out of the boat when I first responded to God's subtle voice. I sensed God whispering that word to me when I felt a clear calling to serve Him in full-time ministry. Just like with Peter, there were no instructions. Just a confident assurance that I was supposed to get out of the boat.

I grew up as a PK (pastor's kid). That moniker is synonymous with trouble. I was told from an early age that I was *destined* for ministry. Before I was born, my parents believed God said I would follow in my dad's footsteps into ministry. This calling was so clear to my parents that they named me Timothy. My dad's name is Paul. If that connection doesn't make sense, read 1 Timothy 1:2 and you'll see the lightbulb moment my parents had for my name.

My entire childhood, I was reminded of this impending doom. At least that's how it felt to me. I was to follow in the family business — God's business. I felt trapped! I ran from this calling, and for a season of my life, I even ran from God. At my high school graduation, I remember being upset thinking everyone else gets to become what they want and I have to become a pastor. Thanks a lot, God!

That is, until I heard just *one word* from Jesus. When I experienced His voice for myself, it changed everything. It was a Thursday night, and I was at band practice for our worship team. Something changed in the atmosphere and, somehow, we ended up in a quiet moment of prayer. I was on my knees with my head on the floor when I heard the whisper from the waves. *Come.* It wasn't so much that I heard an actual voice. But I knew Jesus was calling me onto the waves. It was like a seed of faith was deposited into the soil of my soul, and it was only a matter of time before I would have to harvest it.

Since that night, my journey has been filled with many get-out-of-the-boat moments. Some closer to the shore where I might be able to swim back if I sink, and others so far out into the deep that I will drown if God isn't with me. And when it comes to walking on water, every time feels like the first time.

Maybe you're in your own "boat" right now, just trying to survive a storm. Perhaps you feel less like Peter and more like the other disciples hiding in the bottom of the boat. Maybe you're in a storm because of some bad decisions or because you've run away from God. The good news is that Jesus will still show up in that kind of storm, too! Just ask Jonah from the Old Testament. He sailed into a storm because he tried to run away from God's calling. Yet God met him in the middle of his storm with grace the size of a whale. He's the God of second chances.

Would you allow me to speak directly to your soul right now? Would you permit me to speak something over your future? It doesn't matter why you are in a storm, all that matters is what you *do* in the middle of it. Either you respond to the voice of Jesus calling you to Him or you keep rowing your own direction using your own strength. Can I encourage you to respond to His invitation? He's inviting *you* to step in His direction. He's inviting you to take a step of faith.

So, I ask you, have you heard that voice calling out to you?

If not, could I challenge you to make some room for God to speak to you before you read the next chapter? I believe God is always speaking to us. We just need to make listening for Him a priority.

Let me give you a few thoughts to get you started.

- Shut out all the distractions of your day and get alone with God.
- Ask Him what He wants you to do, and then listen for a small voice reflecting off the waves.
- Tell God your wildest dreams for serving Him with your life.

- Write out your passions and dreams for serving God. (Don't limit it to what you think you could accomplish. Be bold. Be brave.)
- And then, be ready to listen. (Oh, and you might need to focus your mind and spirit like this for a season before you hear Him clearly. But trust me, He will answer you.)

When it comes to hearing God's voice, I've never heard it audibly. But I'd sure love to! For me, it's almost always an inner thought or feeling that is so strong I can't shake it. And sometimes it will happen when you least expect it, like at band practice. You'll know when it happens. Something inside of you catches fire.

It's exciting and terrifying at the same time.

It never comes with clear instructions.

It's an invitation, not a command.

It's always just one word.

Come.

3

FIELD OF DREAMS

"All men dream, but not equally. Those who dream by night in the dusty recesses of their minds, wake in the day to find that it was vanity: but the dreamers of the day are dangerous men, for they may act on their dreams with open eyes, to make them possible."

~ *T.E. Lawrence*

I F YOU BUILD IT, he will come.

I still hear the angelic whisper as Kevin Costner stares at a cornfield. I'm talking about the epic 1989 movie, *Field of Dreams.* At this point, you are going to think I'm way older than I really am with these classic movie references. Would you believe I was just a kid when this movie came out?

Field of Dreams is the story of a farmer in Iowa named Ray who hears a voice one day telling him to build something. He takes it as a sign to build a baseball field in the middle of his farm. Knowing it may bankrupt his family, he can't help but respond to the voice. He thinks by building this baseball field his childhood hero, Shoeless Joe Jackson, would somehow return from the past to play baseball again.

Several times throughout the movie Ray hears this voice encouraging him to go the distance. He builds the baseball field and then deceased legends of the game show up to play baseball nearly every night. The deeper storyline is that it was really about Ray reconnecting with his late, estranged father, who shows up to play catch at his magic field. And sure enough, with a fitting storybook ending, people lined up for miles to pay money to watch a magical baseball game with legends of the past.

The farm is saved.

The dream becomes a reality.

A perfect Hollywood ending.

This movie has captured the mindset of every developer, entrepreneur, risk taker, and church planter. Everyone who is brave enough to start something that could fail has taken considerable risk with these words echoing quietly in their soul.

If you build it, *they* will come.

It's this hopeful expectation that if you step out in faith, your dream will come true. If you start the business or begin the venture, it will succeed.

Speaking as someone who started a church, I know the sentiment.

A lot of people have dreams. A lot of people will also grow old wishing they had chased their dream instead of staying in the boat. Many dreams have died on the plains of regret having never been planted.

There's something that separates people who have dreams and those who build baseball diamonds in the middle of a corn field. You must be more than a dreamer if you want to change reality.

Perhaps that's the difference between dreamers and builders. Dreamers *see* a picture of what could be. Builders *create* the picture they see. If you are going to turn your dream into reality, you have to be willing to get out of the boat.

Maybe that's why I like Peter so much. I'm not sure if any of Jesus' disciples besides Peter even wondered if they could walk on water. Peter didn't just see Jesus on the water; he saw himself on the water. Perhaps the rest of the disciples were too embarrassed by the yellow stain on their pants to even consider standing up in this moment.

DREAMERS SEE A PICTURE OF WHAT COULD BE. BUILDERS CREATE THE PICTURE THEY SEE.

Before I had a church, I had a dream. I dreamt of a church that would be different than what I had previously experienced. I wanted a church for people who didn't go to church. I wanted the kind of church where the irreligious could find their way to Jesus. I wanted a church that wasn't fixated on religious traditions but an authentic experience with Jesus. I dreamt of a church that would see thousands of people find hope in the same grace I had received.

It was this dream that birthed our church.

It was a dream that started in Russia.

Within one year of getting married to my wife, Lorelei, both sets of our parents left the country. My parents moved to an Air Force base in Italy just months after our wedding and Lorelei's parents moved to Russia as missionaries the following year. Keep in mind that we got married when I was twenty and Lorelei was eighteen. Nothing grows you up quicker than having no parental net around when you first navigate adulthood and marriage.

I remember the day Bob and Denise (my in-laws) called and told us they felt it was time to come home. After serving nearly five years in Russia, they sensed God was leading them to a new adventure. We were thrilled to have parents living in the same state with us again! We just had no idea God was going to include us in their new adventure. I can still remember the moment they asked us this exciting but scary question, "Do you guys want to start a church with us?"

I had basically grown up in one church my entire life. I had never thought about starting a church before and had zero experience planting a church. Yet, something inside of me jumped at the idea of creating something new. I had grown frustrated and discontent with my church experience.

Don't get me wrong, I loved the people of our church. But something was missing. It wasn't anything like the raw unbridled gritty experience you read about in the book of Acts. We weren't reaching people who needed Christ. The vision wasn't clear, and I was drifting. It felt more like an exclusive club than a messy community of grace. I wanted something more.

For two years, we dreamed about the church we would one day build. We got together weekly and took walks around our neighborhood praying, talking, scheming, and dreaming. Every dinner, every hangout, turned into a dreaming session. We dismantled previous methods of church, tore down cultural barriers, and sketched with our imaginations.

We dreamed with our eyes open.

———————————

There is something exciting and fresh about dreaming. No resources. No limits. Just creating the world we want to see. We were building an imaginary church world before Minecraft was a thing. That's the beautiful thing about dreams — they are filled with endless possibilities. Lack of money, facilities or personnel doesn't affect your dreams. The only box you live in is the one you've created.

It costs nothing to have a dream.

It will, however, cost you everything to build it.

Perhaps you have an embryonic dream forming in the recesses of your temporal lobe even now. You have an idea that could alter the course of history or, at the very least, your future. Or maybe you don't feel like you even have the seed of your future growing inside your soul. You've wrestled with the feeling that you are supposed to do something more with your life but aren't even sure where to begin. All you know is that life has to be about something more.

I believe many people today are not living up to their full potential. Not because they aren't working hard or aren't successful in life, but because they aren't doing what God created them for. It's easy to forge your own path in life without stopping to ask God what direction He wants you to go. So many are hacking their way through life only to end up missing the destination God intended.

If you don't have a dream inside of you, why not begin asking God to give you one? If you aren't sure how God can use you, then start by asking Him to show you.

Here's what I know. In Jeremiah 29, God gives a promise for those who want to discover Him.

> You will seek me and find me when you *seek* me with all your heart.
>
> [Jeremiah 29:13 emphasis mine]

Although this was originally spoken to the nation of Israel, I believe that same promise extends to all of us. God is not playing cosmic hide-and-go-seek with us. God longs for us to look for Him. He has left clues throughout the universe hoping we will follow the breadcrumbs and find Him. He's a Father who desires nothing more than for His children to want to be with Him.

Here's what I've discovered in my life. When you search for God, not only will you find Him, but also His plan for you. You will never discover God's purpose apart from Him. But something incredible happens the moment you pursue God. Your life intersects with His Spirit and fills you with new inspiration and fresh vision. That's when the words of prophet Joel come alive for us.

> "And afterward, I will pour out my Spirit on all people. Your sons and daughters will

prophesy, your old men will dream dreams,

your young men will see visions."

[Joel 2:28]

This is when we begin to dream with our eyes open. This is when God begins to illuminate our path in life. This is what enables you to hear the voice of God whisper, "If you build it, they will come."

And when you hear it, you can't unhear it.

Once you feel it, you can't ignore it.

You have to pursue it.

You have to look fear in the eyes.

You have to step over the side of the boat.

Things got real on February 22, 2002. That's the day our dream became incorporated in the State of Ohio. Paperwork was filed. We were officially a church!

Of course, that wasn't the dream. Anyone can do that with $125 and some paperwork. But somehow it validated the dream. For our small team, it set things in motion that could not be stopped. One way or another, we were going to see this dream come to life.

By the end of that year, we found a small storefront in a newer industrial park that we could afford to rent. We had 3,000 sq. ft. of blank canvas in front of us. All we needed to do now was paint with some lumber, drywall, and nails.

On weekends, our small group of five guys, mostly family, would go to work turning a small open warehouse into our field of dreams. The entryway opened right into a small auditorium that held about seventy banquet-style chairs. To the left of the stage was a single door into our open and spacious children's ministry floor plan. That's a generous way of saying we had a single room for kids of all ages.

After months of construction, we were finally ready for the inaugural day. The launch codes had been set for Easter, April 11, 2003. Years of planning, praying, and financial investments were finally going to pay off. Finally, we were about to see this dream go from a whisper to a baseball game. We were ready for the steady stream of headlights just like in the movie, *Field of Dreams*. We built it, now they will come. Right?

The only challenge was that we really didn't know how to launch a church well. This was before there were as many tools available to church planters as there are today. We invited all the people we knew in our town. We went door-to-door with our nearby neighbors, letting them know about this new church that would change their lives. Most were polite and thanked us for the invitation. Who knows, they were probably thinking, *there goes the neighborhood!*

We placed an ad in the local newspaper, thinking that would get the word out quickly. It was going to be our mass announcement to the community. That was until I found out the newspaper ran the ad in the *wrong* community paper. To say I was upset would be an understatement.

Not only was I nervous about our opening day, but I was also preaching my first Easter message and only my fourth message ever. I was new to church planting and equally new to preaching. As I look back now, it was the perfect setup for a major letdown.

I was in my mid-twenties and had zero pastoral experience. My wife's parents were in their forties and had a lot. The original plan was for Bob to be the lead pastor and eventually hand it over to me. Afterall, the idea of planting a church was originally theirs.

Then one day, about a year before we started the church, Bob and Denise approached me and my wife while we were in our cramped, poorly wallpapered kitchen. Lorelei was cooking dinner while I talked her ear off, as I so often would do. They said they wanted to talk with us about something important. Immediately, PTSD set in from the last time they had something important to tell us — that they were moving to Russia!

"Tim, we think you are supposed to be the lead pastor now," Bob proposed with Denise shaking her head in agreement.

Though I was shocked to hear them say it, something inside of me agreed.

"I think I'm supposed to be too," I blurted out.

I sure hope that didn't come out sounding presumptuous. I just felt inside that God had called me to be the pastor. At the time, I had no idea what I had gotten myself into.

Launch day finally arrived, and my stomach was a mess. There is something scary about putting your dream in a position where it will either succeed or fail. Those moments are so emotionally charged that we rarely forget them. I have never forgotten exactly how I felt that day.

I've heard so many successful church planting stories in recent years. New churches launching with hundreds of people attending on their opening day. Church plants that turned into medium-sized churches overnight. I wish I could say that was our story, but it wasn't even close. On opening day, we had *one* family show up from the ad that went in the wrong newspaper.

One family.

I was hoping our first day would be more like that final scene in *Field of Dreams* where cars lined up for miles to be on the ground floor of this explosive vibrant move of God. Instead, one car showed up. No one cued the cinematic music. It surely didn't look anything like what I had been seeing in my dreams. I've long thought if you consulted church planting experts, they would agree that church planting wasn't for me.

As I reflect back on that moment, perhaps I had a bit of a build-it-and-they-will-come mindset. Perhaps I was too inexperienced to know better. I had never planted a church before, and I didn't know what it would take to make it successful. Perhaps life's greatest lessons are learned through painful failures, not easy successes.

My grandparents had an incredible reminder of this truth sitting in their house. Every time we visited them in Virginia, I would admire a trophy that reminded me of my legacy. My great-grandfather, Benjamin B. Lipsner, received a prestigious award for starting something new. He is credited for starting *airmail* in the US. Perhaps now when you receive an electric bill or birthday card in the mail, you will think about my family. Though this might not seem impressive to us today, it was quite a feat over a hundred years ago. So much so, the trophy my great-grandfather received came directly from Orville and Wilbur Wright. I'm sure you are familiar with the story of these brothers from Dayton, Ohio. Their dream paved the way for us to do the impossible — fly.

The Wright brothers developed a prototype of a manned glider that would hopefully defy gravity and return to the earth in one piece. Their first attempts in 1900 and 1901 failed miserably. Back to the drawing board. Yet, despite numerous setbacks, the Wright brothers refused to leave their dream on the ground. They would create a flying machine, even if it killed them. In fact, it was so dangerous that their father, Milton, made them promise to never fly together. He was afraid he would lose both of his sons to this dream.

Finally, their dream took off on December 17, 1903, in Kitty Hawk, NC. For an entire twelve seconds, Orville piloted a propelled bi-plane 120 feet and safely landed on terra firma. Perhaps you are tempted to think that's not much of a feat. But if it had not been for those few aerial seconds, you and I may not be able to spend twelve hours in a plane soaring 35,000 feet above ground. Their tenacity to not give up on their dream created a better future for all of us.

Two things we must consider before we turn a dream into reality.

First, just because you build it doesn't mean they will come.

Just because you start something doesn't mean it will be immediately successful. The day you open your new store people might not line up around the block to visit, though I hope they do.

However, *until* you start building it, your dream will *never* come true. Until you sign the lease, take out the loan, or pick up a hammer and nails and get to work, your dream has no hope of getting off the ground.

See, fear will ground you. It will keep you dreaming with your eyes closed.

So, open your eyes and take a step.

The sad reality is that *Field of Dreams* is probably a better metaphor for the place most dreams are buried. It's not the location for a new baseball field, invention, business venture, or even a church, but rather the plot of ground where dreams lie grounded. It's the place where we never took a risk. The inside of the boat.

If you want to live your life with *no regrets*, you'll need more than a bad tattoo around your neck. You need to respond to the voice you hear in the wind. It requires you to reach for the edge of the boat, lift your leg over the side, and shift your weight onto the water.

In that moment a rush of thoughts will flood your mind.

What are you doing?

You can't float.

You will drown.

Get back in the boat.

But if you are determined to create a new future, you must step into the scary process. Every second you remain in the boat is another delay from your God-given destiny. Perhaps God is calling you out on the water with Him today.

What dream do you need to put action behind today?

What step could you take today that would initiate your dream?

What would you attempt right now if you knew you couldn't fail?

What excuses have you been telling yourself so you can remain in the boat?

I'm believing that in this very moment, the voice of God is calling to you over the water. He's saying, "Come." He's inviting you into a greater story. But like Peter, He's waiting to see if you will step over the side of the boat.

Second, turning a dream into reality is a *process*.

It won't happen overnight. There are no overnight successes. In our culture, it's easy to get jealous of another person's highlight reel. We see someone's influence or budget and wish we had their platform or resources. The problem is we often see the accomplishments, but rarely see the late nights, sacrifices, and personal pain they went through to create the success. It's the

Iceberg Effect. What you see is only about ten percent of what someone has endured to build it.

People that come to our church today see the result of nearly twenty years of investment. The amount of blood, sweat, tears, and money that I and many others have given to see this vision come to life is incalculable. We didn't take over a church with a budget, building, and resources. We built it from scratch.

It takes time to build your dream into reality. Don't get so impatient that you walk away from your fledgling startup because it's hard. Don't quit before the seed has enough time to germinate. If it was easy, others would already be doing it. And if you sense God is leading you to do something, it becomes a matter of obedience.

IT TAKES TIME TO *BUILD* YOUR DREAM INTO REALITY.

Oh, and one more thing. The more significant your dream is, the more it will cost you to bring it forth. The bigger the dream, the greater the challenge to create it. And remember this, every big dream has a small beginning.

Do not despise these small beginnings, for the Lord rejoices to see the work begin, to see the plumb line in Zerubbabel's hand."

[Zechariah 4:10 NLT]

God rejoices to see the work *begin*. I love that! God celebrates the start of the process, and so should you.

It's work. It's hard. But it's part of the process that God wants to build *in* you and *through* you. Trust me, one day through the years of sweat and heartache, you will discover the real joy is in the journey, not the success.

So, what dream is hiding in your heart? What audacious goal have you been putting off? What excuses have grounded you before the inaugural flight? Before you move on to the next chapter, think of *one* step you can take to begin building your dream, today! Write it down. Now show it to someone who will keep you accountable.

You have to build it brick by brick. There are no shortcuts.

You have to build it *before* they will come.

So put your shovel in the ground and start digging.

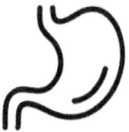

4

GOD OR GUT

"Is God's voice the loudest voice in your life? That's the question.
If the answer is no, that's the problem."

~ Mark Batterson

NIKOLA TESLA WAS POSSIBLY one of the most brilliant inventors in the late 19th and early 20th Century. Most accredit Nikola with the invention of alternating current (AC) power, something we all use every day. I bet you've also heard of the *Tesla* coil. Yup, that was Nikola, not Elon Musk. But perhaps the most significant impact of Nikola's work was in the field of wireless radio transmission. Though he never got the support needed to create half of the inventions he dreamed up, he did claim something rather interesting.

Nikola claimed to be the first person to receive contact from outer space. In 1901, Nikola believed he was being signaled from another planet via his radio telegraph. Here is an excerpt from an editorial piece printed January 13, 1901, in *The Times* (Richmond, VA).

"As he sat beside his instrument on the hillside in Colorado, in the deep silence of that austere, inspiring region, where you plant your feet in gold and your head brushes the constellations — as he sat there one evening, alone, his attention, exquisitely alive at that juncture, was arrested by a faint sound from the receiver — three fairy taps, one after the other, at a fixed interval. What man who has ever lived on this earth would not envy Tesla that moment! Never before since the globe first swung into form had that sound been heard. Those three soft impulses, reflected from the sensitive disc of the receiver, had not proceeded from any earthly source. The force which propelled them, the measure which regarded them, the significance they were meant to convey, had their origin in no mind native to this planet."1

Tesla was convinced he received communication from an extraterrestrial source. Though he was never able to identify the source of those three taps, we can never rule out that someone or something was trying to reach us.

Of course, I could argue that I too have received communication from an extraterrestrial source. Meaning, I've had moments I was certain that I heard from God. Perhaps you have too.

The Bible is full of such moments. Some people even claim to have heard God's audible voice. Though I have never heard God speak audibly, I do believe He often speaks to us in a still small voice from within. The challenge is, and always has been, identifying the *source* of that voice.

This was the disciples' challenge. They were convinced they saw extraterrestrial life in the middle of a storm. In the pitch-dark, with waves crashing over the side of their boat, they saw an image walking toward them on top of the water.

"It's a ghost!" they cried.

That's when they received this vague communication echoing off the waves.

"Take courage! It is I. Don't be afraid."
[Matthew 14:27b]

I laugh inside every time I read this account. It seems as though Jesus was trying to calm them down. This is exactly what you would say to someone who is freaking out. But I'm not sure Jesus was really helpful in this particular moment.

Let me put this response into perspective for you. Imagine you are awakened out of a deep sleep to a strange noise coming from outside your house. You get up and try to turn your lights on only to find the power isn't working. As you peer out the window to see what is causing the noise, you catch the glimpse of a silhouette moving near your garage. Being either brave or stupid, you open the backdoor and say, "h-h-hello?"

Only to hear a voice from the shadows reply, "Don't worry, it's just me."

Me?

Who is me?

I don't know what I would think if I saw a ghost and heard it say, "Don't worry, it's just me." I would have at least needed a name! It might have been far more helpful if Jesus had said something like, "Hey guys, it's me, Jesus! I know you're freaking out right now, but I wanted to ride along in the boat and didn't have any other way to get out here." But he doesn't.

I'm not quite sure why Jesus doesn't make Himself clearly known in this moment. Perhaps He figures His disciples should recognize the sound of His voice by now. Or it could be this is how God *often* speaks to us.

Have you ever felt like you heard from God? I know I have. But often I know it only because something confirms it after the fact. In other words, it's usually only clear God was speaking to me *after* He climbs into the boat. But when He is still in the shadows out on the water, that's when I find myself trying to decipher His cryptic messages.

One of the questions I've been asked frequently as a pastor is how to know if you're hearing from God. I believe many authentic Christ-followers want to go where God is leading them.

They want God to speak to them and guide them. Usually, I get these questions when they have a major life decision to make.

There is a misconception that pastors have a special phone in their office with a direct line to God. Let me dispel this myth right now. There is no God phone in my office! In fact, I don't have *any* phone in my office. But I get it. I, too, struggle to know if what I'm sensing is from God or just my gut.

God, are you leading me to change careers, or am I just bored with my life?

God, are you wanting us to move to another state, or is that just something we want to do?

God, are you encouraging us to adopt or try infertility treatments again?

This is the internal conversation most Christ-followers have whenever they are unsure of God's will. My guess is you have possibly had this same internal dialogue when you felt uncertain of your next move. We want to know if Jesus is really out there *before* we move in that direction. Why? Because we don't want to step outside of God's will. We know God's blessing only comes when we walk *with* God. It's scary whenever we step in a new direction. And knowing we're in God's will gives us a sense of peace about an otherwise uncertain decision.

I can't tell you how many times I've struggled to identify the voice of God over my years as a pastor. I'm the leader and *expected* to know where we are going. People are looking to me for direction. I'm supposed to know what to do next. I feel this pressure constantly.

I wish I could tell you that being a pastor made it easier to hear God's voice. But I have the same challenge all of us do — attempting to decipher those three taps on my spiritual radio device. Trying to figure out if it was God or the pizza I ate the night before. The truth is, God's voice sounds an awful lot like my thoughts. Everything you process must run across your prefrontal cortex, including His voice.

Recognizing God's voice is as complicated as the circuitry of our brains.

———————————

The human brain fascinates me. The way a brain works to initiate ideas, form thoughts, and respond to others is marvelously complex. Let's consider for a moment how this happens in the physiology of our brains. Sound exciting? I can picture you now on the edge of your seat just hoping we'd talk some neurology.

Small nerve cells known as neurons are believed to be responsible for originating ideas or thoughts. When neurons *fire* they generate electrical signals through neurotransmitters which sends the message to other neurons.2 This message is called an *action potential*. I love that term because every idea formed has the potential of action with it. This network of neurons engages the prefrontal cortex to process the thought for a response.

Your prefrontal cortex is like the command center for your ideas and thoughts. It engages other parts of your brain to formulate cognitive thoughts and then processes a response by sending a signal to your motor cortex. Your motor cortex is responsible for initiating gross and fine motor skills throughout your body. Peter used fine motor skills when he spoke back to Jesus and gross motor skills when he stepped over the side of the boat.

But something else happened before Peter would decide to step over the side of the boat. Peter had to determine if the voice he heard was from Jesus or a ghost. You see, it was dark, and Peter and the other disciples were unable to identify Jesus by sight. Perhaps this is why Peter asked a question in response to hearing the voice from the waters.

"Lord, *if it's you*," Peter replied, "tell me to
come to you on the water."

[Matthew 14:28 emphasis mine]

Peter clearly could not see Jesus' face nor recognize His
voice in the storm. If we broke this moment down into physics, it
might sound like this: sound waves from Jesus' voice passed
through Peter's ear canal, vibrating his eardrum. The vibrations
from his eardrum then got amplified along three tiny bones and
went to the cochlea, a snail-shaped structure filled with fluid in
the inner ear. The vibrations created small, wave-like ripples in
the cochlea's fluid which then brushed against hair cells. When
these cells got excited, they sent an electrical current of neurons to
Peter's prefrontal cortex.3 The prefrontal cortex then sent neurons
to other parts of the brain that held a catalog of voices and faces
looking to match the voice with a face. Either there was no match,
or the storm interfered with Peter's ability to verify based solely on
the voice pattern.

Let me guess, that's probably what goes through your
mind every time you read this passage, *huh?* The point is,
recognizing God's voice is more complicated than we would like
it to be.

If Peter struggled to recognize Jesus' voice in the storm, how much more difficult is it for us? Peter had an advantage. He knew what Jesus' voice sounded like. Peter heard Jesus speak so much his brain had cataloged Jesus' voice pattern.

God has pre-wired our brains to recognize speech patterns and tuck the information away in a repository. We match the sound we hear with the visual image we see, and it creates a form of *Caller ID* for our brains. The more we hear a specific voice and match it with a single source the better we are at recalling it, even if we can't see the person speaking.

My wife's late grandmother, Dollie Sykes, was diagnosed with Alzheimer's Disease near the end of her life. We noticed signs of her memory deteriorating whenever we visited. Dollie would forget that my wife was married to me and what I did for a living, even though I had been her pastor for many years! She lost her ability to recognize our faces and the sound of our voices. It's quite sad when someone you know so well doesn't know you anymore.

Even though those years were quite hard, I have never forgotten the day my wife and I visited her in the hospital. She knew right away who Lorelei was, but I could tell she wasn't sure about me. Her nurse walked into the room and Dollie began bragging about her granddaughter. She kept saying over and over how her granddaughter was such a good girl.

"What about this guy?" the nurse belted out, referring to me.

Dollie looked up at her and without skipping a beat said, "Well, I don't know if he's good or not, but he sure is good looking!"

She was the best.

I believe our ability to recognize faces and voices is *critical* to how God made us. Without this feature we would struggle to develop authentic relationships with anyone. Basically, every day would be Ground Hog Day when it comes to people we meet, including our grandkids.

Dr. Claudia Roswandowitz, a research scientist in the field of auditory cognitive neuroscience, discovered the area of the brain responsible for voice recognition storage. She and her team discovered that patients with lesions in the right posterior temporal lobe had trouble recognizing even familial voices. Those patients had what is known as *phonagnosia* — loss of voice recognition.4

Here's what I'm saying: learning to recognize God's voice is much harder when you haven't seen His face or heard His voice before. I've never seen God or audibly heard Him. I'm assuming you haven't either. You and I have nothing in our catalog to match against the inner voice we hear. We are living with *phonagosia* when it comes to recognizing God's voice.

As we discovered with my wife's grandmother, losing your voice-identity recognition can cause you to lose trust in the person behind the voice. And when you consider that the way we most often *hear* God's voice is through a thought forming in our prefrontal cortex, you can understand why we question where it comes from. Let's face it, you and I have a lot of thoughts to parse through every day.

According to a study by psychologists at Queen's University in Kingston, Canada, humans typically have about 6,200 thoughts every single day.5 No wonder it's so hard to recognize the voice of God. Not only do we have to wade through the thousands of thoughts fluttering through our neural networks, but we also don't have any voice-recognition software to apply to the source of the thought. It's easy to understand our confusion when trying to figure out if a thought originated from within us or from God's mouth.

So, you can imagine how difficult it is to make faith-filled decisions based upon *hearing* the voice of God. Like Peter, before I get out of the boat, I want to know it's Jesus calling me and not some crazy idea I concocted. Unfortunately, God rarely gives us the perfect calling card. Usually, His invitation is a bit vague and uncertain. Often, it's just a notion, a feeling, or a burden.

And it might seem crazy to everyone around you.

———————

Over the years leading our church, I've faced several moments where I questioned if I was hearing from God. I have led our church through multiple capital campaigns and cast a vision so big that it's embarrassing to even think about. I was young, passionate, and full of ambition. I am still just as ambitious today, only I have a few more wrinkles of wisdom from walking through some scary faith decisions. In every one of those situations, I've questioned whether or not I heard from God when making a hard decision. Oftentimes, the only way you will know for sure that you heard from God will be after you obey Him.

Perhaps right now you are facing your own major life decision. It could be a decision to change careers at an older age or leave gainful employment to start your own business. Or maybe you're facing a monumental decision to move back home to care for your aging parents. Perhaps you're wrestling with the financial decision to quit your job and stay home to raise your kids. You aren't sure if you can make it financially, but you feel this strange desire pulling you from the inside. You are left wondering if this idea came from God or your gut — from heaven or your own passions and pursuits.

If so, my guess is the weight of this decision hangs on you like a freshman's bookbag. It's hard to walk on water when you feel so heavy. You know that making the wrong choice could have serious consequences. You could lose your house or end up filing for bankruptcy if it all goes south. Or at the very least, you might embarrass yourself in front of your friends and family. How do you tell your children there's no money for new school clothes or, even worse, why you have to move to a smaller house and put them in a new school district?

I know the tension of being in this kind of place. It's scary! And sure, it might be faith, but it's definitely not fun. Sometimes I even wonder if God enjoys watching us squirm or if there's a greater plan at work. It seems as though God leaves out a lot of details when He calls us to live by faith. I'm even starting to wonder if He does this on purpose.

God didn't give Abraham the address of his new home. He just told him to pack a U-Haul truck and move his family to an unknown destination (Genesis 12:1).

God didn't give Moses details on how to bring the Israelites out of Egypt. He just sent him to confront the Pharaoh to rescue His people (Exodus 3-4).

God didn't give Peter lessons on water walking. He just invited him to get out of the boat (Matthew 14).

For whatever reason, you'll find this pattern whenever God calls people to take a step of faith. Often, it's just a one-word command.

Go.

Speak.

Come.

Maybe God doesn't give us the end picture because He wants us to rely on Him through the process. Perhaps if God gave us all the details, we might not ever choose to move.

If Abraham knew how many miles he would have to travel, he might have opted to stay put.

If Moses knew how hard the journey through the wilderness would be, he might not have answered the call.

If Peter knew he might sink, he probably would have never responded to Jesus' invitation.

And maybe if I knew how many times God would ask me to lead our church to take risky steps of faith, I would still be working with routers and switches.

The question is, will you move on a single word from God?

Even if that word is *perhaps*?

That's all Jonathan had when he made the scariest decision of his life.

In 1 Samuel 14, we find the Israelite army cowering in fear from their archrivals, the Philistines. Saul, the commander-in-chief, was camping under a pomegranate tree rather than engaging in the battle. However, his son Jonathan knew in his spirit that someone had to take action to turn things around.

WILL YOU MOVE ON A SINGLE WORD FROM GOD?

Without his father's knowledge, Jonathan grabbed his armor-bearer, the guy who carried his shield and sword, and decided to advance against an outpost themselves. They would be outnumbered and outgunned. Between the two of them, they only had one sword. You can probably guess who got to use the sword.

What you find in this passage is possibly the greatest dichotomy of fear and faith at play. While Saul was frozen in fear, Jonathan made a bold faith move. He risked his life on a *perhaps*.

> Jonathan said to his young armor-bearer,
> "Come, let's go over to the outpost of those
> uncircumcised men. *Perhaps* the Lord will
> act in our behalf. Nothing can hinder
> the Lord from saving, whether by many or
> by few."
>
> [1 Samuel 14:6 emphasis mine]

Perhaps?

Really?

Put yourself in the shoes of Jonathan's armor-bearer. Your leader just asked if you would go with him on a suicide mission on a *perhaps*. He might as well have said, "Let's throw ourselves in front of a moving train and see if God stops it for us."

We don't even know that God spoke to Jonathan like he did to Moses through a bush or Samuel in a dream or Peter on the lake. We aren't told that Jonathan heard a *word* from Yahweh. All we know is that Jonathan knew God was on their side and someone needed to have enough courage and faith to act.

It takes unbelievable *courage* for two guys with only one sword to advance on twenty armed combatants. And it takes faith to do it on a *perhaps*. *Perhaps the Lord will act on our behalf.* Jonathan knew God was *able* to save them, he just didn't know if God *would* save them.

What is not to be overlooked is that amount of faith that *both* of these men had. Jonathan and his armor-bearer might have only had one sword, but they both had faith! One could make an argument that the armor-bearer might have had even more faith than Jonathan.

> "Do all that you have in mind," his armor-bearer said. "Go ahead; I am with you heart and soul."
>
> [1 Samuel 14:7]

Here's some insight: the armor-bearer was the one getting into a swordfight — *without a sword*. But he knew he wasn't going into the fight empty-handed. He had God on his side. And together, he and Jonathan believed God would perform a miracle on their "perhaps" faith.

You see, this is the essence of faith. Remember our earlier definition? Faith is the confidence of what you hope for and the assurance of what you do not see. What this doesn't define is exactly how *much* confidence or assurance you have. The truth is, we will almost never have full assurance of *anything* God asks us to do. If we did, then it's not faith or God.

The real question is, exactly how much assurance do you require before you will take a step of faith? Do you need 90% assurance that something will work before you get out of the boat? How about 75%? What if you only have 51%? What will it take before you are willing to risk it all to follow God's voice?

When our little team of three families started our church, all we had was a *perhaps*. When I asked our small church to give sacrificially and risk financial viability to buy the property in Lithopolis, I only had a *perhaps*. I wish I could tell you that I had 100% assurance it would work. But to be honest, I only had about 51% faith that it would work.

By the way, I never had a visitor from heaven instructing me on what we should do. God never appeared to me in a dream with a plan for growing our church. All I had was an invitation to follow Jesus and a sense that this is what God wanted us to do. That, and the hope God would act on our behalf.

Jonathan turned his "51% faith" into a miracle. He and his armor-bearer attacked a regiment of twenty Philistines soldiers and — with the grace of God — killed every single one of them. They moved on a *perhaps* and God moved on their behalf. Their bold step of faith caused panic to set in among the Philistines and changed the outcome of the war.

YOU WILL NEVER *WALK* ON WATER UNTIL YOU HAVE THE POSSIBILITY OF *SINKING*.

If you need 100% assurance before you step out, don't expect to see miracles. You will never walk on water until you have the *possibility* of sinking. You have to get out of the boat first. Then, and only then, will you see God's miraculous power in your life and step into the life you never imagined possible.

So, what is God prompting your heart to do for His kingdom?

What would you attempt for God if you knew you couldn't fail?

Is there any area of your life where you have resisted God's voice out of fear?

If you honestly don't have any clue what God might be calling you to do for His kingdom, then I would encourage you to go back over the end of Chapter Two. Use those tools to help you learn to hear God's voice. You will have to eliminate distractions and posture your heart to listen intently. At first, that can seem challenging. But over time, if you will respond in obedience to even the slightest prompting from God, you will train your spiritual ears to pick up the vibrations from heaven.

But for those of you who know the answer to those questions already, I strongly encourage you to make a move, even a small move, today! Write it down and post it somewhere that will constantly remind you. Stick it on your bathroom mirror or computer monitor. Also, tell someone you trust and ask them for accountability and help. Let a pastor or mentor know what God has put in your heart and ask them for guidance. Then, give yourself a deadline to act.

Just do something.

Because if you ignore the voice of God enough, eventually you will stop hearing it altogether. Far too often we ask God to answer our voice when we pray, but then haven't answered His voice when He prompts. Some of us don't need to listen for God to speak. He already did. And until we are obedient to what He has already asked us to do, we shouldn't expect Him to say more. In God's eyes, true success is *obedience*, regardless of the outcome.

Will you move on a *perhaps*?

5

BLACKJACK FAITH

"A life without risk is a life without meaning."

~ *Erwin Raphael McManus*

FREDRICK (FRED) SMITH WAS born with the odds stacked against him. He had a rare birth defect that caused severe arthritis in his hips affecting his ability to walk. Though resigned to using crutches and leg braces for much of his youth, he was determined to walk and did just that by the time he was ten. In fact, he went on to play football and basketball in high school.

Fred was always fascinated with flying. By the time he was a teenager he had his private pilot's license. After graduating high school, he attended Yale University where he majored in Economics, but kept his sights on the sky. In 1966, Fred wrote a term paper on the economic benefits of using air transportation to deliver packages overnight rather than ground transportation. Though he can't remember for sure, he's almost certain he received a *C*, which was his usual term paper grade.

After two tours in Vietnam, Fred bought controlling interest in an aviation company and decided to put his concept to work. In 1973, Fred started *Fed Ex* with the rest of his four-million-dollar inheritance. He also procured another 80 million through loans and investments. With financial backing, *Fed Ex* got off the ground with eight planes servicing just thirty-five cities.

Fred soon discovered his idea of turning a profit through air transportation would prove more difficult than he'd imagined. The company was losing money every year, and with rising fuel costs, bankruptcy was starting to look like a real possibility. Some of his pilots were charging fuel on their personal credit cards while others were holding uncashed paychecks.

Finally, staring at a $24,000 fuel bill with only $5,000 in the bank, Fred decided to do something not only risky but what many would call foolish. He took a flight to Las Vegas where he proceeded to gamble the remainder of the company's cash. That evening Fred turned $5,000 into $27,000 playing blackjack! And with that, he was able to pay the fuel bill and keep the company in operation for one more week.

Considering this to be a sign, Fred went to work raising another $11 million to keep the company afloat and by 1976, the company turned its first profit — $3.6 million. Today, *Fed Ex* is a publicly-traded company that is worth an estimated $73 billion. *Gulp!* Not bad for a C-grade idea.

Behind nearly every success story, you will find someone who was willing to *risk everything.* Fred not only risked his own life savings; he convinced others to do the same.

UNTIL YOU ARE READY TO *FAIL,* YOU AREN'T READY TO *SUCCEED.*

The truth is you will rarely accomplish anything *significant* without taking *significant risk.*

Until you are ready to fail, you aren't ready to succeed.

Disclaimer: please do not take this as a sign from God that you are supposed to fly to Vegas and belly up to the high roller table. For every story like this, there are surely fifty other stories where people have lost everything. Yes, there's something about gambling that brings a real rush of adrenaline. The thought that you could hit it big or lose it all with the flip of one card is both scary and exhilarating. But there's a reason why Vegas boasts billion-dollar hotels and casinos. Let me put it this way. Casinos aren't losing money!

———————————

Several years ago, my wife and I went on a cruise with some friends. My friend — we'll call him Jay — was a bit of a gambler and would often bring stacks of cash on vacation to have some fun at the blackjack table. After a string of bad luck, he found himself down about $2,500. Jay decided to do something bold. He grabbed another $2,500 out of the cabin safe and decided to risk it all with one final bet. He figured he would either break even or lose it all. If he was going down, it would be in a *blaze of glory* as they say.

We entered the casino like we were headed to the playground for an after-school fight. Pulse racing and adrenaline pumping, we walked straight up to the pit boss. Jay flashed some cash and next thing we knew, a young woman with brown hair and fair skin emerged from a mysterious door in the back of the casino and proceeded to open a private table for him. I felt like we were in a movie.

The dealer pulled out the fresh deck of cards from the tumbler and after a few extra shuffles, she handed him a red card to split the deck. Jay pulled a wad of bills out of his pocket and threw twenty-five hundred-dollar bills on the table. My heart was racing, and I didn't have a single penny in the wager.

In blackjack, your cards are dealt face up so everyone can see them. Meanwhile, the dealer has one card face up and the other down. The goal is to have a higher pair than the dealer without going over twenty-one.

The cards were dealt, and the dealer was showing a three. That's not a great card for the House, but it's a good sign when you are playing *against* the House. Jay shocked me when he tapped the table, signaling he was taking a hit (asking for another card). He had twelve on the table and the dealer was holding a bust card.

I leaned over, "You sure you want to take a hit?"

But he just looked at the dealer while tapping his finger. "Give me another one."

The tension was thick. The dealer slid another card from the shoe and flipped it over. A six. A wave of relief came over us both. He began waving his hand over the table indicating he was staying. He held at a respectable eighteen. All the sounds of the casino evaporated in that single moment. I thought to myself, "He might just do this."

The dealer flipped over her face down card. A ten. With only thirteen in hand, the dealer had to take another card. The odds of her busting (going over twenty-one) were pretty strong. Our eyes were glued to her hand. The room fell silent. The clinking of the slot machines ground to a complete halt. All I could hear was the thumping of my heart. In what felt like slow motion, her hand reached for another card and flipped it over. Our eyes zoomed in on...

A seven.

Noooooooo.

The dealer had twenty!

My stomach and his head dropped. Within a matter of two minutes, he lost everything. Although it wasn't my money, I understand why they call it the thrill of victory and the agony of defeat. We made the walk of shame and didn't set foot in the casino again for the rest of our trip.

Let me again throw out a disclaimer, lest I be labeled "reckless" for writing this chapter. This is *not* an endorsement to risk your future at a blackjack table. But I do believe risk and faith are intrinsically tied together. You can't separate the two.

Unfortunately, that is what we have so often done in Western Christianity.

We want a safe God who will make our lives comfortable. Many are willing to follow Jesus as long as it doesn't cost them *too* much. There is a version of Christianity that believes God's primary goal is to make you safe, comfortable, and prosperous in life. Yet, when I read stories of the people who responded to God by faith, I find the exact opposite to be true.

God asked Jonah to preach destruction to his enemies.

God asked Moses to leave his family behind to confront the Pharaoh.

God asked Elijah to pronounce judgment on Israel at the risk of his own life.

But we really don't have to look any further than Peter. He placed the ultimate bet when he asked Jesus if he could join him on the water. While it would have been much safer to remain in the boat and wait for Jesus to come to them, Peter decided walking toward Jesus was worth the risk of drowning.

His faith wouldn't allow him to remain in the boat.

I'm convinced many Christians today are willing to follow Jesus as long as they can remain in the boat. We grip the side of the boat to keep ourselves *inside* of it, resisting the possibility of what could happen outside of it. The moment Jesus calls us to something we've never done before, something that seems scary or perhaps even impossible, many decide to sit crisscross applesauce on the bottom of the boat.

My father-in-law used to always say, "Faith is spelled R-I-S-K!" I think he's right. We like to think we are *all in* until it costs us everything, or even just something. Yet, we must remember this is exactly what Jesus said it would cost us to truly follow him.

> Then he said to them all: "Whoever wants
> to be my disciple must deny themselves and
> take up their cross daily and follow me.
>
> [Luke 9:23]

Some think this verse means they should wear a sterling silver cross around their neck (if it matches their outfit). But I believe the power of this statement has been lost in our modern world. In Jesus' day, the cross was one of the most frightening images. It was by far the greatest form of torture and death the Roman Empire implemented. It wasn't just about the excruciating death, it was also about the message it sent everyone else — don't cross Rome.

Jesus said if we truly want to be His disciple, we must choose to daily put to death our desires. In other words, until you are ready to surrender it all, you aren't ready to follow Jesus.

I will admit it's hard for us to identify with this idea of sacrifice and risk. We live so carefully that to do anything overly risky feels irresponsible at the very least. But might I humbly suggest, sometimes faith looks a little irresponsible.

I remember the first time my wife and I had a risky faith decision to make. In January of 2007, my church leadership team suggested I leave my full-time career in Information Technology and step into full-time ministry. It was something I had always hoped would happen, but when the option was put on the table the decision got scary.

We wrestled with the decision to leave a great career in a stable workplace with full benefits to step into something unknown. At the time, our small church consisted of about sixty adults and twenty children on a good Sunday. I knew there was no turning back if the church failed or if it couldn't afford to pay me a salary. It was hard enough to get hired by the State of Ohio the first time, and nearly impossible to get rehired.

I had plenty of reasons to worry. I had always heard around eighty percent of church plants failed within five years. It hadn't even been four years. Questions flooded my mind as I processed taking the risk. Would the church be able to afford my salary? How would we carry benefits for our family since the church couldn't afford to provide them?

My IT career was the boat. Full-time ministry was like walking out on the water.

It wasn't that we didn't believe God could provide or that it was His will for us. It's just scary to step into something unknown where there's a significant risk of failure. Fear of drowning will always keep us inside the boat.

I knew my wife and I had to be in full agreement to make this big of a decision. I'd like to say we had been praying about it for weeks but, honestly, we had been wrestling with fear for weeks. I was ready to take the step, but she wasn't quite there yet. Not until she heard God speak to her 30,000 feet above the earth.

We were on our way back from a church leadership conference in Texas. Freshly inspired and full of faith, we sat in our cramped seats reflecting on the past few days. I was dreaming about all the changes I wanted to implement so our church could reach those who are far from God. Lorelei was reading her Bible in the seat next to me.

Then suddenly she leaned over and whispered, "Okay, I'm in. Let's do it."

I believe there is power in confirmation when stepping out in faith, and she finally had hers. God spoke to her the moment she read Jesus' words found in Luke 9.

> Jesus replied, "No one who puts a hand to the plow and looks back is fit for service in the kingdom of God."
>
> [Luke 9:62]

It was time to put our hands to the plow.

No looking back.

Get out of the boat.

I went to work the next day and put in my notice.

———————

On April 1, 2007, I drove to the church rather than to my former downtown office. It was surreal. It was exciting. It was scary.

It was also April Fool's Day, and I couldn't help but wonder if I was the fool.

I'm not going to lie, my first year in full-time ministry was one of the hardest. I struggled in the transition and became increasingly frustrated that nothing seemed to be happening. I took long prayer walks every day and had it out with God. I lost my appetite and twenty-five pounds. I'm not sure if I was clinically depressed, but I was certainly discouraged.

I thought to myself, "Why did I walk away from a career I loved for this?"

Something was wrong.

Our church had stopped growing due to many limitations. We had expanded our facility three times, but it still wasn't a good place for families with kids. The parking was inadequate and, I have to admit, the location was terrible. Something needed to change, but I didn't know what to do. That's when Rob Slane, a guy on my leadership team, suggested something crazy.

"I think we need to find a new location," he blurted out.

He was right.

We needed to move.

We looked for buildings to rent, but nothing was viable. One day, my office administrator, Joy, showed me an old, deserted church building on twenty-one acres in a nearby town. It wasn't ideal, but we were getting desperate to find anything that would work. That is until we found out they wanted $1.5 million for it. We were a small church with probably no more than $15,000 in savings.

We decided to get a realtor and walk through the building anyway. We learned that the previous congregation had dissolved due to a major rift. It got so bad that the pastor locked the front door with a chain in the middle of the week.

I'm not sure if it's possible for a church building to have bad mojo, but this one was giving off a scary vibe. It was quite eerie walking through an abandoned church building that was still set up from its Sunday services four years earlier. I imagine it was like walking through an old movie set from the *Left Behind* series.

Knowing they were dissolving a non-profit organization, we made an embarrassingly low offer of $250,000 for the entire property. In our minds that was all we could afford.

The seller never responded.

I'm pretty sure we insulted them with our offer.

A few days later, I wrote in my prayer journal, *God if you want us to have that property, change their mind.* Less than two weeks after I started praying that prayer, their realtor reached back out to make a counteroffer. They would accept $750,000 for the building and five of the twenty-one acres. That amount still seemed beyond what we could handle, but it was a very fair price for the property. We countered by offering the full $750,000 for the building and *entire* twenty-one acres. We truly believed our vision was bigger than five acres could hold. We needed it all.

I was on pins and needles waiting for their reply. Part of me was hopeful, the other part not wanting to be let down again. I remember the exact moment the email from their realtor came.

I was holding my breath while I opened it up. Then a smile streaked across my face.

They accepted our offer!

I couldn't believe it.

God truly answers prayers.

We got it! I was thrilled, elated, and beaming with excitement. And that's when reality hit me like a two-by-four to the side of my head. Once again, questions.

How in the world could we afford this? We didn't even have money in the bank for a down payment.

How could we afford the bigger payment?

How could we afford to pay the mortgage *and* our salaries?

I had no idea. All I knew is it felt like something we were supposed to do.

———————

One thing I've learned about walking by faith is that you often find yourself facing insurmountable odds.

Like David marching out to face a giant or the prophet Elijah squaring off against 450 prophets, you will always feel overwhelmed by the odds. And yet the reason we know their stories is because they risked everything. We worry about risking our financial stability or reputation, but these men risked their lives. If God did not come through for them, they would not have survived.

All I can tell you is the line between faith and stupidity is very blurry. What feels like faith to you might look ridiculous or even irresponsible to someone else. It's hard to know if you are making the biggest mistake of your life or watching your greatest miracle unfold.

THE LINE BETWEEN *FAITH* AND *STUPIDITY* IS VERY BLURRY.

But you will never know until you try.

Someone needs to hear this. Some of the things God will call you to do will *not* make sense. Some of the things God puts in your heart will *not* seem possible. People might think you are crazy or even irresponsible. You will even be tempted to believe them. But this is the space of faith.

Remember, faith is spelled R-I-S-K.

Now, please don't go and do something reckless and blame it on faith. Don't quit your job just because you feel inspired right now. Don't cash in your 401k and start that lemonade stand idea you've had for forty-five years because I'm saying faith requires risk. There is a difference between *calculated* risk and *obedient* risk. Perhaps we could use some clarity from Jesus himself.

In Luke 14, Jesus noticed a crowd of people had started following Him. Huge crowds gathered around Him because He healed the sick and performed miracles for them. This particular time Jesus sensed the crowd's motive for being there was insincere. Often when this happened Jesus would say some challenging things to test the purity of their devotion.

To paraphrase, Jesus tells the crowd unless they are willing to give up everything, including their own family, they cannot be His disciples. The language Jesus uses is quite abrasive. He then restates the very words we read earlier in Luke 9:23. Nothing short of daily sacrificing your life qualifies you to be Jesus' disciple.

But then He continued by posing a question about sensibility and risk. Listen to this warning Jesus gave them.

"Suppose one of you wants to build a tower. Won't you first sit down and estimate the cost to see if you have enough money to complete it? For if you lay the foundation and are not able to finish it, everyone who sees it will ridicule you, saying, 'This person began to build and wasn't able to finish.'"

[Luke 14:28-30 NIV]

At first glance it would seem like Jesus is against taking risks. I think we'd all agree it's definitely wise to calculate the cost before you attempt something new. You should have all the materials or the funds before you start building a house. Anything less would be irresponsible. But to apply this broadly to faith is to miss the point entirely.

Jesus wasn't discouraging people from taking bold steps of faith. That runs counter to the very concept of faith. Jesus often invited people to leave everything behind to follow him. That requires *bold* faith. In this passage, Jesus isn't talking about faith, he's talking about the *cost* of faith.

Following Jesus isn't like holding your hand out waiting for God to drop blessings from heaven. That's a perversion of the truth. It's about putting your hand to the plow to risk and sacrifice your life to advance God's kingdom.

Before we take even a single step in His direction, we should know what we have signed up for. Jesus finally makes it clear in verse 33.

> In the same way, those of you who do not
> *give up everything* you have cannot be my
> disciples.
>
> [Luke 14:33 NIV emphasis mine]

The truth is most people want to follow Jesus as long as it doesn't cost them *too* much. They will follow Jesus as long as He heals their marriage, but not if it requires having to leave their high-paying job. They are *all in*, until they are challenged to give ten percent of their income to their church. They are good to talk to Jesus on Sunday, as long as they don't have to talk to their co-worker about Him during the week. In truth, this mindset will never lead us to the same place Jesus is going. Only when we have a willingness to give up everything are we truly ready to follow Jesus wherever He leads.

Until I was willing to give up my reputation, my income, and my ministry, I wasn't ready to go where Jesus was leading me. I also wasn't able to receive what Jesus was offering.

Unfortunately, I believe there are many pastors and leaders in the Church who have gotten so comfortable in the hull of the boat they aren't willing to risk walking on water. We can easily fall into the trap of *babysitting* God's Church rather than *advancing* God's Kingdom.

Instead, we keep telling ourselves there is too much to lose.

I agree. The problem is we don't realize what is really at stake. It's not our reputation or career that is at risk. It's the lives of an entire generation of people who are lost without Christ. It's more than that. It's also our God-given purpose and destiny that is lost when we slump back down into the boat and bury our heads in fear.

This isn't just seen in the Church. It's seen in every facet of business. The larger an organization becomes, the harder it is to make risky decisions. An entrepreneur starting out has nothing to lose and everything to gain. But the leader of a multimillion-dollar organization with hundreds of employees has a lot to lose.

When the fear of loss is greater than the pain of remaining where you are, you will rarely take risks.

Read over that statement again and let it sink into your spirit. When the fear of loss dictates your life, you will become complacent in a mediocre life void of new fruit. You will live in the past, reveling in the "glory days" instead of stepping into an unlimited future of possibilities. You will become all too familiar with *lukewarm* living.

You need to know Jesus despises lukewarm coffee. Who doesn't, right? Probably everyone except the woman who sued McDonalds for selling her scalding hot coffee. Most people only want their coffee hot or iced, not lukewarm.

My guess is that Jesus doesn't care about the temperature of our coffee, but He *does* care about the temperature of our passion. He cares about the ferocity by which we follow Him. We get this truth from Jesus' own lips to John's ears when talking about one of the early churches.

> I know your deeds, that you are neither cold
> nor hot. I wish you were either one or the
> other! So, because you are *lukewarm*—

neither hot nor cold—I am about to spit you
out of my mouth.

[Revelation 3:15-16 NIV emphasis mine]

I wonder if Jesus views many western Christian churches today like He did the church in Laodicea. It's far too easy to say you *follow* Jesus but not actually *go* anywhere. To reduce faith to a set of beliefs we hold rather than a call to get out of the boat.

When was the last time you said to yourself, "If God doesn't show up, I'm going to fail"?

When was the last time you took a big risk in your faith?

When was the last time you gave more than you felt comfortable giving?

When was the last time you responded to that internal nudge to lead something you felt inadequate to lead?

When was the last time you attempted something so scary it drove you to your knees?

These are very real questions. And I don't want to downplay the fact that many have tried and failed. If we are going to put ourselves in that kind of position, we better stay as close to Jesus as we can. I seriously doubt Peter stepped over the edge of the boat and then took a step *away* from Jesus. The reality is, living by faith will be a daily reminder of your dependence on God.

Perhaps the greatest benefit of living out on the water is we must remain close to Jesus.

The moment I signed the contract for the property, I realized how much we needed God to show up. The bank told us we needed $125,000 down before they would loan us the remainder. And we only had a couple months to raise it or the contract would expire. I had never led a capital campaign before, but that wasn't going to stop me from trying. To some this might not seem like a lot of money, but for a church that brought in roughly $3,000 per week in the offering, it might as well have been a million dollars.

We tried every old-school method of raising money you can imagine. We asked people to donate unwanted jewelry and we sold the gold for cash. We hosted a blues benefit concert and sold tickets to raise money.

I even held a golf-a-thon! Most people walk or run dozens of miles. I wasn't about to do that. But I loved golf, so I figured, why not play it to raise money? I asked people to sponsor me for every hole of golf I could play in a single day. I played eighty-four holes in just one day! I have no idea what my score was but, trust me, I didn't want to play golf again for a long, long time.

To this day, I'm still not quite sure how it happened.

Families gave money they had saved for vacation.

One college student gave $5,000. (And I'd thought all college students were broke!)

Another woman received a settlement from an injury accident that left her with chronic pain. She tithed on the settlement just weeks before we closed on the loan. I don't believe God was behind the accident, but I do believe God was in the timing of the settlement.

All I know is God showed up when we stepped out in faith.

On May 30, 2008, we became the proud owners of a thirty-year-old outdated church building with a gravel parking lot so steep you could go sledding on it in the winter. As you walked up the enormous concrete steps with rickety metal handrails, you felt like Rocky training to fight Apollo Creed in Philadelphia. The small lobby had a metal spiral staircase that ascended to the haunted attic... sorry, I meant to the sound room. The sanctuary had blood-red carpet and the stage had two white pulpits. I believe the larger pulpit was for the pastor while the lay people reading

Scripture used a lesser-anointed pulpit. Maybe they were on to something.

Even though it was incredibly dated, the building had a bit of traditional charm to it. The pews and stained glass windows took you back to that old-time religion. The problem was our church wasn't about old-time religion. We had a dream to reach people who were disenfranchised with church. We set out to create something different with hopes of reaching people in a new way. This building did not match that vision. So, with our small army of church volunteers, we started our own version of *Extreme Church Makeover*.

That summer we did pretty much everything ourselves. We didn't have money to hire professionals. Someone graciously donated new concrete steps to make this unfriendly building a little more inviting. We tore out all the pews and old carpet and installed new carpet and chairs. We built a new stage and sound booth, and we gave the lobby a fresh makeover. We took a risk and — gasp! — covered the stained-glass windows and painted the ceiling dark.

Some people got mad and left the church.

We were shrinking before we even opened.

We spent many Saturdays and late evenings ripping out walls, patching holes, and slapping paint on everything.

The basement was our new kids ministry area, and we all felt uneasy tackling it. Old metal tables and chairs were still setup with crafts placed neatly for children who had never gotten to use them. We knew the pastor had chained the front door four years earlier so no one could use the building. And now, it literally felt like the rapture had taken place and everyone was gone — but us! It brought back memories of those scary '70s rapture movies I was forced to watch in youth group. I didn't sleep for days after watching them. Nevertheless, we mustered enough courage to disturb the crime scene and created some semblance of a kids space.

At this point, we had a small budget of around $20,000 left from our savings to update the entire building. This wasn't even *close* to enough.

We ran into unexpected plumbing and electrical issues that required licensed contractors. By the time we were done slapping *lipstick* on everything, we were way over budget. Not only did we just take on a loan that more than tripled our rent, but we also ended up with credit card debt of more than $20,000. This was not from irresponsible spending, either. It was simply unrealistic to turn that building into something that resembled our vision. We had underestimated the job.

It's safe to say we were *all in*. There was no Plan B if this didn't work. It had to work. If we didn't grow to cover the increased expenses, I was out of a job, and we were out of a place to gather.

But what happened on September 14, 2008 will be sealed in my memory forever.

When you put everything on the line and lead people to invest their savings into your vision, you get more than nervous. You get downright sick. And I guess you could say I was dealing with morning sickness that day, pregnant with expectation, the dream inside making me want to fly and vomit at the same time.

Finally, I got the courage to head upstairs and slip out onto the newly-cemented front porch. I couldn't believe my eyes.

Narrator: *Tim blinks multiple times and then rubs his eyes.*

A stream of cars lined our thousand-foot drive with traffic backed up to the main road. My heart skipped a beat or two. I don't even remember who was standing next to me, but choking back tears I said, "Where are all these cars coming from?"

For the first time in a long time, I could finally take a breath. For me, this was the closing scene of *Field of Dreams*, only people weren't coming to a baseball game. They were coming to our church.

Then the thought hit me, "Oh no, I have to preach to all of them!"

Our first day in our new building, nearly three hundred people showed up and five people dedicated their lives to Jesus. We scrambled to add more beige banquet chairs to our tiny but packed auditorium. The energy in the room was palpable. It felt like something was happening.

Oh, that's right. Something *was* happening!

For months leading up to that day, I had questioned over and over whether this was the best or worst decision of my short ministry career. Flashbacks of our launch in 2003 when only one family showed up drowned my mind in the days leading up to that Sunday. This was the first time I put myself in a situation where if God didn't come through, I would fail.

Listen, I'm not an adrenaline junkie, but this moment was both exhilarating and terrifying at the same time. This was me, putting both soles of my feet on the water and stepping away from the boat. It still ranks up there for me as one of the greatest moments of my spiritual journey.

Faith often feels this way. It's stepping over the side of the boat hoping for spiritual buoyancy. In the natural, it rarely makes sense. To an outsider, it may look reckless. You will question your decision over and over until it either works... or fails.

Most people think faith is a category of belief or a religious affiliation. But real faith will release adrenaline, make your heart race, and leave you desperate for God. You won't know what it's like to feel faith until you can feel the water beneath your feet.

Good news, though. That's also when you feel the most alive.

6

OPPORTUNITY DOESN'T KNOCK

"Chance favors the prepared mind, and opportunity favors the bold."
~ Louis Pasteur

MOST PEOPLE HAVE NEVER heard of Ronald Wayne. Ronald was born in Cleveland, Ohio in 1934. He eventually moved to California and started a company selling slot machines. The company failed within five years, and he went to work for Atari. In 1976, Ronald helped form a small startup company with two twenty-year-olds both named Steve.

These young passionate computer enthusiasts had a lot of technical knowledge and ideas, but very little experience running a company. They struggled to agree on the direction of their business, so they invited Ronald to be a third partner for ten percent equity in their company. He was added to the team to bring "adult" supervision.

Ronald went to work drafting their partnership agreement, drawing the company's first logo and writing a manual for their first product. He got nervous, however, when one Steve took out a line of credit to fulfill a purchase order for computers with a company that had a bad reputation for not paying. The memory of his failed slot machine company was still haunting him. After only twelve days with this startup company, Ronald decided to cash out his share of the company back to the programmers for $800. He didn't want to expose himself to the possible risk.1

Today, ten percent of Apple's stock would be worth more than 100 billion dollars. That's "B" as in b-b-billion. Ronald slipped onto the pages of obscurity when he passed up this once-in-a-lifetime opportunity. I think we could all agree he sold too soon!

There's an old proverb that says *opportunity never knocks twice at any man's door.* Perhaps you've heard it more commonly expressed, *opportunity only knocks once.* I love the urgency and passion of this statement. If we don't seize every opportunity that presents itself, we could live full of regret. We could end up like Ronald. I believe there may be no poison more deadly to the human spirit than *regret.* No one wants to look back on life and think, "if only I had..."

On the other hand, I've had my fair share of regrets when I seized opportunities that came knocking on my door. In my early twenties, a co-worker introduced me to a family friend who managed a small investment fund. It was a private fund, yielding between ten to twelve percent. *Monthly!* We are talking over a hundred percent return on your investment in just one year. It was an exclusive, private investment opportunity and my co-worker could get me in on it. To put a cherry on top, the investor was a Christian — which made him instantly more trustworthy to me. It was almost too good to be true (I'm sure you can see where this is going.)

I not only invested most of our humble savings, I also convinced my parents and my brother to invest thousands of their savings as well. The first few months we saw between five and seven percent returns. At this point, I was trying to figure out how to retire by age thirty. For a hot minute, I even considered taking out a second mortgage to invest in this once-in-a-lifetime opportunity.

Am I glad I didn't.

After a couple of months, we stopped receiving our regular monthly email updates. Probably the spam filter, right? Nope, I checked. No emails. Perhaps he was just too busy making bank to send us statements. I sent him emails but received no response. I asked my co-worker if he had heard from our private moneymaker, but he said he hadn't heard anything either. Something was wrong. I could feel it.

We eventually found out our so-called-Christian investment manager had a gambling problem. I don't mean he was a little too risky on the market. I mean he spent too much time at the horse track. He gambled away more than 2.5 million dollars of personal investments. At one point, I heard he had some unsavory folks (probably named Guido) who were looking to break his legs or worse. Not sure why I think Mafia bosses are named Guido. Perhaps out of fear of ending up at the bottom of a lake, he turned himself in and pleaded guilty to embezzlement charges.

All the money was gone. All *our* money was gone. We might as well have lit our cash on fire and roasted marshmallows over it. Part of his sentence was to repay all the investors. Every few years I receive a check from the probate office for about nineteen dollars. I can't help but chuckle when I get those checks. Perhaps my grandkids will get the final restitution payments.

My point is not every opportunity that lands on your front door is one to be seized. We should always use wisdom when making significant decisions. If FOMO (fear of missing out) drives our decision making, we are likely to lose a lot of money, time, energy, or relationships. Perhaps what we want to know is how to make sure we don't miss out on the opportunities *God* wants us to walk through.

Christians love to talk about open doors. Typically, we associate an open-door opportunity as something God *wants* us to do. If the door swings open to an opportunity, it must be God, right? And if we don't find any open doors in front of us it must mean God doesn't want us to move forward. We can easily reduce our faith to a formula of open or closed doors.

However, before we attribute every open door to a Divine Locksmith, we may need to apply prayer, wisdom, and counsel. After all, I walked through an open door and lost our savings. Based upon this simplistic logic, I'm left with only two options for seeing my investment woes. Either God wasn't on the other side of that open-door opportunity or God unlocked it to teach me a lesson. Not sure either conclusion should be on God's shoulders. Perhaps the problem was my lack of due diligence before I invested.

The reason we love to rely on the open-door method is because it makes hard decisions easier. Rather than wrestle with every opportunity through prayer, fasting, and truly seeking God for clarity, we reduce our decision-making to finding the one unlocked door. We turn faith into fate. We might also prefer this approach because it gives us a sense of *certainty* in the face of uncertain decisions. It builds a plank onto the boat, so we don't have to get our feet wet.

I like that.

But that's not faith.

Because faith *lives* in uncertainty.

The other danger of reducing faith to fate is we can be tempted to blame God when we make the *wrong* decision. It's much easier to pin my decisions on a Cosmic Janitor who holds all the keys. But this is potentially dangerous to one's faith. If we walk through the wrong door or feel we made the wrong decision, we are likely to determine that either faith doesn't work or worse, God doesn't work. Both of those conclusions leave us completely unsettled.

Though I certainly believe God will make a way for whatever He is calling you to do, I also believe we have to exercise faith to *find* the God opportunities in front of us. What I'm saying is you might have to go looking for the door God wants you to walk through. You might have to actively seek out God's direction for your life and not just assume every open door has been unlocked by God.

I'm reminded of the promise God spoke to Israel through the prophet Jeremiah.

> You will seek me and find me when you
> seek me with all your heart.
>
> [Jeremiah 29:13]

Please don't misinterpret this verse to think God is playing a cosmic game of hide-and-go-seek with us. What God desires is for us to want *Him* and not just what He can do for us. He wants us to pursue Him by faith, not just assume we will find Him by walking through open doors. I'm convinced God cares far more about us *seeking* after Him than He does which door we walk through.

Perhaps this is what separates walking by faith from working by fate. Fate assumes God is behind every open door. The reality is, you have probably walked through some doors that were popped wide open and found they led you further from God. If you leave decision-making up to fate, you may end up somewhere you never wanted to be. Faith, on the other hand, is learning to trust God's voice, wherever it leads.

FATE ASSUMES GOD IS BEHIND EVERY OPEN DOOR.

Perhaps even now as you read this, you have felt something inside of you kick. There have been moments when you felt a nudge toward the edge of the boat, but you are still waiting for a sign or a door to hit you when God swings it open. I would argue, perhaps God already has.

Could something like this be *growing* inside of you?

You have a desire to start a business that would bring real change to our world.

You have a nagging feeling that you are supposed to downsize your lifestyle to become more generous.

You feel the pull to mentor someone younger, perhaps someone at your church.

You can't shake the thought you are supposed to take a medical mission trip and serve the impoverished with your skill.

You feel drawn to go back to school and change careers to find your passion.

These desires to do something with meaning or to create something impactful are the seeds of purpose God has deposited in you. Some are pregnant with God-given vision and don't realize it. And sadly, the dream isn't developing and the vision isn't growing because many are *waiting* for a sign from heaven. I'm convinced there are many who will never step into their God-given purpose because they don't activate their faith to *find* the opportunity.

We're waiting on God.

God's waiting on us.

Stalemate.

Maybe you should consider God putting the inspiration inside of you *was* the first move. What if God dropped the vision in your heart, and now He's waiting for you to *activate* it with your faith? The inspiration is there. All that's missing is the perspiration.

Isn't that what Peter did?

Peter didn't secretly hope Jesus would invite him to moonwalk the waves. In fact, I'll bet if Peter had never said anything, the story might have ended with Jesus walking up to the boat, everybody making room for him to climb into it, and the storm dying down.

The End.

A miraculous moment for Jesus.

But not for Peter.

Now, if we look closely at this story, we might determine that Peter *opened* the door for his opportunity to walk on water. Peter spoke up first. He didn't wait for Jesus to offer an invitation; he invited himself into the miracle. He knew Jesus could walk on water but wanted to know if *he* could walk on water, too.

"Tell me to come to you on the water."

[Matthew 14:28b]

This is Peter seizing the moment.

This is Peter turning the doorknob with his faith.

Rarely will opportunities knock on your front door like Ed McMahon delivering a Sweepstakes check. That's a reference for my more experienced audience. If you sit around waiting for miracles to fall out of the sky, your spirit will die a slow death in a recliner. That's like praying to God for a girlfriend and sitting on the couch clutching your phone just waiting for Ms. Perfect to call. But then again, who answers calls from unknown numbers? I guess if God really sent her your number, she would most likely leave a message.

Better check your voicemail.

————————————

In the life of our church, the greatest miracles we've experienced didn't happen because we got a random email or phone call or because one day someone knocked on our door and said they felt compelled to give us a million dollars. Though, I will say, I'm still holding out hope that may happen! Most of the *God moments* came because we tried opening a lot of doors, hoping one of them would be divinely unlocked.

The building we purchased in the sleepy town of Lithopolis happened because we went looking for our next step.

In fact, we had to look really hard for it because I'm not sure Lithopolis even shows up on Google Maps. It was so easy to miss, I almost missed it. It took real eyes of vision to see what it could be. I remember driving on the property for the first time thinking this looks like the perfect setting for a B-rated horror film. But we also saw it as a potential door we could walk through.

We turned the doorknob.

It opened.

God was there.

Shortly after we moved to Lithopolis, our church exploded in growth. Within only a couple of years, we had more people attending our church on a weekend than actually lived in the town of Lithopolis. Lives were changed. Hundreds were baptized. No one in the church knew this, but I secretly prayed in 2007 that our congregation would double every year for three years.

It did.

Only God.

I wish I had prayed for more.

Maybe we need the same urgency as the two blind men who happened to be in the right place at the right time. They were hanging out just outside of Jericho when a mob of people overwhelmed them. I'm not sure if they got nervous from the crowd bumping into them, but they must have heard the murmur of Jesus' name mentioned over and over. Surely, they knew the story of this Nazarene who healed people just like them. And now Jesus was passing by right in front of them.

This was their opportunity.

But Jesus didn't stop.

No one knocked.

Matthew tells us these two men were not going to miss their chance. They stood up as tall as they could and started shouting to get Jesus' attention.

"Lord, Son of David, have mercy on us!"
[Matthew 20:30b NLT]

The crowd of people tried to shut them up. Surely it started with scowls, but that didn't affect them. The blind men just kept yelling for Jesus. People in the crowd were getting annoyed with the loud outbursts and collectively tried to silence them (that culture was brutal toward people with disabilities.)

> But they only shouted *louder.* "Lord, Son of
> David, have mercy on us!"
> [Matthew 20:31 NLT emphasis mine]

Good thing they didn't give up because this opportunity would have been lost forever. No one was aware of what was about to happen to Jesus. Only Jesus knew He would never walk those steps again. He was on the way to Jerusalem for the last time. Just days after this, Jesus was arrested and killed on a cross.

Jesus heard their desperate cries over the chaos of the crowd and stopped to ask them what they wanted Him to do for them.

> "Lord," they said, "we want to see!"
> [Matthew 20:33 NLT]

They got their sight.

Opportunity seized.

Door unlocked.

Somehow, despite my lack of experience, our church continued to grow after we moved to Lithopolis. We expanded our facility two more times over the next four years. We then launched another location in Lancaster, a town twenty minutes away. We had simply outgrown our building in Lithopolis. I knew we needed to find something else or we would remain stagnant. I thought, *I've been down this road before.*

I spent days driving around with my executive pastor looking for property to buy or buildings to inhabit. We called several property owners and even looked at a warehouse, but nothing felt right. We met with some developers to pitch an idea that would put us in what seemed like a prime location. But it fell on deaf ears. After weeks of restless driving and calls with realtors, we were cruising down Diley Road, and I said, "I'm tired of trying to kick down doors."

My spiritual leg was tired.

That's exactly what it felt like. It was as if I was the proverbial door-kicker for God's SWAT Team. I was determined to find an *open door* by straight-leg kicking every door until I found one that popped off the hinges.

Sometimes we can be so eager to *find* an opportunity that we have to be careful we don't *create* the wrong opportunity. Like the Old Testament prophet Jonah, you can always find a ship heading in the wrong direction. I want to be sure it was God who turned the small latch in the doorknob when I finally get to open it. I also want to know God is on the other side of whatever door I walk through, and my guess is you do too. Otherwise, you might bust through the wrong door only to hope God sends a huge fish to save you from drowning.

I'm not sure what is worse — missing a God opportunity or kicking down the *wrong* door. I know neither of these options is what we want. In my years as a pastor, this is often the greatest fear people face when seeking guidance. Often the fear of choosing the wrong door paralyzes too many.

Most people think fear causes only two primordial responses. Fight or Flight. Your amygdala, a small almond-shaped section of your brain, releases chemicals in a perceived fearful situation to help you focus on survival. We'll dive more into this concept in a later chapter.

I have personally witnessed the power of the amygdala in my oldest daughter, Lauryn. She usually exhibits the *flight* response when she sees even the tiniest of spiders. I think she has a legit arachnophobia. I've never seen her go to battle with one of those menacing eight-legged creatures that is 1/100th of her size. When she sees any size spider, her amygdala lights up and it always results in a blood-curdling scream, like someone just got their arm chopped off. Mind you, this is not a Braveheart war cry mustering the troops to fight to the death. This is her, "I'm about to be attacked by a swarm of tarantulas from the movie *Arachnophobia,*" cry as she runs in the opposite direction with her hands flailing in the air. I'm sure you get the visual. She has a healthy amygdala.

But there's a third and possibly deadlier response to fear — freezing. It's when you are so overwhelmed with fear that you simply can't move.

Some neuro research has been done recently to figure out why we sometimes don't attack or run away but simply stand still. It seems this kind of response happens when our brain thinks that neither fight nor flight are options for survival. Our brain feels so overwhelmed and trapped in the moment that we can't move.

Perhaps this basic survival instinct is the reason we don't step out in faith when faced with an *uncertain* outcome. Perhaps we find ourselves freezing in the face of fear rather than responding with faith. We may never take *any* opportunity because we fear walking through the *wrong* door. We are frozen by *what if* questions.

What if God doesn't want us to build this new house?
What if this feeling is my desire and not God's will?

What if I take this new job but God wanted me to stay put?

What if I completely miss God?

My guess is Peter probably had similar thoughts in this fearful moment on the lake. I imagine his amygdala was going crazy while he communicated with this ghost. I wonder if Peter went through a litany of *what if* questions as he heard the voice from the waves saying, "come."

What if Jesus can walk on water but I can't?

What if it's not really Jesus out there on the water?

What if some evil spirit is tricking me into my watery grave?

I wonder if a few "why" questions even started forming in Peter's prefrontal cortex.

Why did I open my stupid mouth again?

Why didn't I ask him to verify his birthday or last four of his SSN?

Why am I always putting myself in these positions?

All we know is Peter didn't allow fear to dictate his future. Peter didn't remain frozen in the hull of the boat. He slowly lifted one leg over the side and stepped out in obedience.

If you ask me, choosing *no* door is worse than choosing the *wrong* door. I would rather go through the wrong door trying to do the right thing than not walk through any doors. If it comes down to regret or failure — I choose failure every time. I believe regret is one of the worst emotions we can experience. It always seems to haunt you more than other emotions. I could live with failure if I know I gave my best. What I can't live with is not attempting something only to have *what if* seared into my conscience forever.

I want to make sure I have some balance when it comes to the pendulum of opportunity. Living in extremes is always dangerous. I don't want to kick down every door just to cater to my overzealous conquering spirit and become overextended, overwhelmed or worse, irresponsible. And I don't want to live in the camp where I sit around waiting for God to drop a door in front of me with a neon flashing light overhead that reads, "God wants you to walk through this door." Let's be honest, only on *Monster's Inc.* is that even a remote possibility.

What we need is to find a rhythm with the Spirit of God when we pray, look for opportunities, knock on some doors, turn some door handles, and then walk with confidence through a door when we sense God's peace and see His hand.

This is exactly what happened for me with our church.

Shortly after I resigned from God's SWAT Team, things began to move. Even though I quit trying to force my way forward, I still had my eyes open. My executive pastor and I noticed some land in a different area of town that was for sale. It was a large industrial-zoned plot of land near the business district of Canal Winchester, a city near our church in Lithopolis. We set up a meeting with the city's development planner to find out if the city staff would support us pursuing this property. If there's anything I've learned about buying property for a church, it's you better make sure the city staff supports it. If they don't, they will find a way to keep you out.

The development planner would not support our attempt to purchase that property. It was zoned Labor and Manufacturing, and they wanted to bring in that type of business. I picked up from the not-so-subtle hints they didn't want to lose tax revenue on such a big piece of property by allowing a non-profit to build there. Which would have made sense if they weren't offering a multi-decade tax abatement to attract potential buyers.

Door closed.

As we left the meeting with our heads hanging low, we drove past that same property one more time on our way back to the office. Yes, we were kind of sulking in our defeat and the lost dream of what could have been.

On our way by the property, my executive pastor blurted out, "I wonder who owns the parcel right next to this property."

I said something to the effect, "I have no idea and it doesn't matter anyway because it's not for sale."

"I'm going to look it up and call them and see if they want to sell it," he said.

I didn't think much about it after that. I was still wallowing in the face of another closed door. It gets discouraging when you feel like "No!" is all you hear. Then one day, I found out we had a meeting set up with the owner of the property my executive pastor had spotted. Turns out it wasn't for sale, but the owner was willing to meet with us. When we told him we wanted that property to build a church in the heart of a business district, he was surprisingly open to it. He was a fellow Christ follower and loved the idea of a church being in that very spot.

In what I can only describe as miraculous, we ended up buying twenty-eight acres of prime real estate only a couple of hundred yards from the freeway. We didn't wait around for the owner to list the property, we pursued him. I'm not even sure he would have sold it before he passed away (which happened a couple of years later). In the end, we didn't kick down any doors, but we did keep knocking until one opened. We activated our faith but also trusted the leading of God's Spirit.

I like to think that twenty-eight acres wasn't listed for sale because God was saving it for us. We saw God's hand in the entire process. The city was supportive of it. And the seller even put $77,000 in an escrow account to pay for a future tax bill we would be responsible for the moment we developed it.

Only God.

Door opened.

Perhaps we should stop trying to view God's will as a bullseye. I suggest we drop this phrase from our vocabulary: "I just want to be in the center of God's will." Nowhere in Scripture does God invite us to find the *center* of His will. He's not playing a cosmic game of hide-and-go-seek with us. A better picture we find in Scripture is God inviting us into His purpose and then promising to be with us *wherever* we go.

When God installed Joshua to lead the nation of Israel into the Promised Land, He did not lay out an exact plan of how to do it. But He did make Joshua an important promise.

> I will give you *every* place where you set
> your foot, as I promised Moses.
> [Joshua 1:3 emphasis mine]

I love that. God doesn't tell Joshua to make sure he steps in the middle of God's proverbial footprint or else he's on his own. Instead, God gives him something even better — His presence. Not only did God promise Joshua that he could possess every place he walked, but he also told him, "As I was with Moses, so I will be with you; I will never leave you nor forsake you" (Joshua 1:5b).

Wherever Joshua walked, God walked with him.

But it's not just wherever we go, it's also *whatever* we do. We're reminded of this perspective from the Apostle Paul in Colossians 3.

> And *whatever* you do, whether in word or deed, do it all in the name of the Lord Jesus, giving thanks to God the Father through him.
>
> [Colossians 3:17 emphasis mine]

In other words, *whatever* you do, make sure you are doing it with excellence and in a way that honors Jesus. Whatever you choose, it should be something Jesus would attach His name to. Instead of thinking you have to leave the business world for full-time ministry to be in God's will, you can walk confidently in God's will in the middle of the marketplace. And if you feel called to full-time ministry, then begin to look for a pathway toward it and trust God will be with you there too.

Whatever you do — do it for God and it becomes His will for you.

Coaching basketball.

Running a business.

Selling cars.

Staying home to raise your kids.

Pastoring a church.

Again, I feel the need to give a quick disclaimer. Obviously, we can't do *whatever* we want and rubber stamp it with God's approval. We can't choose to live in sin or ignore the promptings of God's Spirit and think we are walking in His will. To do so would dishonor God and be a misinterpretation of this truth.

Do you know what else dishonors God? Doing *nothing*. Living your life in neutral with a fearful spirit will surely keep you out of God's will. Indecision might be the most reckless response of a believer. It leaves us in the very place Jesus loathes.

WHEREVER AND WHATEVER.

Remember what we read last chapter about lukewarm living? The only thing Jesus hates more than rejection is indecision. He would rather you pursue Him with red hot passion or walk away cold as ice rather than do nothing. Strong words. Loving rebuke.

Even now, I hope you can hear the voice of God saying, "come."

Wherever and Whatever.

How freeing is this? Take your hand and swipe the weight from your shoulder! I believe the burden of missing God's will is falling off you right now. You don't have to live in fear anymore that you are going to miss God's will. That is unless you choose to do nothing.

Have you been so afraid to miss God that you stopped taking land for him?

Is fear keeping you from taking a step toward your calling?

Have you been waiting on God so long your faith muscle is beginning to atrophy?

What would you attempt for God right now if you knew you couldn't fail?

I wonder how this opens you up to a world of possibility. May it inspire you to start turning doorknobs or knocking on doors.

Of course, there's always the chance you might fail if you risk getting out of the boat. Peter doesn't know it yet, but he's about to swallow a bit of seawater. Moses ran from his calling after he killed an Egyptian. Joshua failed on his second mission to take over the small town of Ai. But none of those failures meant disqualification. It meant they're human. Maybe we should see failure as part of succeeding. Every person who ever accomplished something significant had to experience some failure.

Perhaps the only way to truly fail is to never take that first step.

7

OPPOSITION IS KNOCKING

"You will face your greatest opposition when you are closest to your biggest miracle."

~ Shannon Alder

T HERE IS NOTHING MORE thrilling that finding out you're pregnant. Okay, I don't know exactly what it's like firsthand, but I remember the moment my wife told me *we* were pregnant. Your entire life changes. You begin to wonder if it's going to be a boy or girl and start a list of possible names and picture playing soccer in the backyard or watching your toddler twirl at her dance recitals.

The hardest part is simply having to wait those forty weeks for the bundle of joy to arrive. Of course, that part was much harder on my wife than it was on me.

Never in those dreams do you picture vents, wheelchairs, or multiple surgeries. Yet that was the reality for my friend Kayla. When she and her husband opted to get a 3D ultrasound, the sonographer noticed something was wrong. She will never forget the uneasy tension that filled the room, the look on the technician's face, or that no matter how many times she asked what was wrong, they refused to answer. Kayla would have to speak with her physician. But in that moment — oh, that eternal moment — she knew her world was about to change.

Odds are that most children are born healthy and without birth defects. There is only a 1-in-33 chance your baby will be born with a single birth defect.1 Kayla's son, Aiden, defied those odds and was born with *multiple* genetic birth defects. The doctors told Kayla if her son survived childbirth, he likely wouldn't live more than a day or two. Kayla determined to love him no matter how long he lived.

Aiden is almost ten years old as I write this. He's a miracle, defects and all. His parents have to keep nearly twenty-four-hour surveillance to make sure his vent doesn't come off or that his airway doesn't collapse. Kayla describes with excruciating detail having to revive him with life saving measures, as if it's a weekly occurrence. He's had thirty major surgeries on his brain, heart, spine, and other major organs. Barring a miracle of near-cinematic proportions, Aiden will never walk, talk, or even know the taste of ice cream. And he's the sweetest boy you could ever meet.

However, Aiden's ability to survive continues to amaze everyone, especially the doctors. And what I'm equally amazed by is Kayla's faith. Her faith has not only survived; it's thrived. She is one of the most joy-filled, hope-filled, and faith-filled people you will ever meet. Not to be too cliché, but she really has managed to turn lemons into lemonade. Kayla has faced more setbacks and challenges in life than I can even imagine. Yet somehow instead of crushing her faith, it has hardened it.

Knock knock...

Who's there?

Opp...

Opp who?

One of life's cruelest tricks is to hear a knock at your door thinking *Opportunity* has come to visit and instead find it's his evil cousin, *Opposition*. I've discovered opportunity doesn't always knock but opposition *is* always knocking at our door. To quote the words of the great poet Edgar Allan Poe:

> ... suddenly there came a tapping,
> As of some one gently rapping, rapping at
> my chamber door.
>
> (Poe, 1845)

This is especially true whenever you step out in faith for God. You will feel the wind of opposition hit you in the face when you move in a direction no one else is going. There's a reason no one is headed that way. It's much easier to open your sails and go with the flow. But if you are determined to do something extraordinary with your life, you had better get used to rowing against the current.

Of course, no one knows that better than salmon. Salmon are one of the few marine animals that live in both fresh and salt water. Salmon are born in freshwater rivers and then make their way downstream until they end up in the ocean. But every year between September and November, an instinct overtakes these fish to return to their place of birth to lay their eggs. They will sometimes travel upwards of 4,000 kilometers to the exact spot of their spawning to repeat the cycle. This is a considerable feat when you realize rivers flow into oceans and not the other way around. That means salmon have to swim *against* the current, leap over waterfalls, and fight for every inch of ground they cover. It's so grueling that very few of them survive trying to return to the ocean after they spawn.

Whenever we feel the internal pull of God's voice to step out in faith, we should not be surprised when it leads us against the current. Let me say it more bluntly. Anything you attempt for God will be met with gale force winds of opposition.

Peter knows this all too well. His first lesson facing the wind of opposition was right here in the middle of the sea of Galilee. Let me remind you what it was like in this moment.

...and the boat was already a considerable
distance from land, buffeted by the waves
because the wind was against it.

[Matthew 14:24]

I'm sure Matthew could recall this moment really well since he was *in* the boat too. The term *buffeted* implies being constantly attacked by the waves. In the original language, this word means "to be tortured and harassed."

Over and over.

No relief.

No escape.

I've never been sailing in a boat at night through a massive storm.

But I have been in a small airplane at night flying through a horrific thunderstorm.

It was one of the scariest moments of my life.

My brother, Peter, was named after Simon Peter in the Bible. However, I'll refer to him as Pete, since he prefers that and it will keep us from getting confused with all these Peters.

Pete's dream was always to be a pilot. After he got his pilot's license, he got a job flying cargo at night. He flew small twin-turbo prop planes to deliver checks to banks and some occasional strange packages marked with the biohazard logo. I don't know this for sure, but I think he transported vials of anthrax or other deadly nerve agents. I guess you could say it makes the job a little more interesting. It's probably a good thing he got out of that line of work since no one writes checks anymore, not to mention the risk of exposure to deadly toxins.

Every so often he would call me up late on a Friday and ask if I wanted to be his co-pilot. I said *yes,* every time! I'm not even sure it was allowed, but he would give me the airport gate code and I would meet him on the tarmac. I know we weren't flying narcotics across the border, but it sure felt like it.

He would let me fly the plane once in the air. I know, scary, right? I figured I would be a great pilot after my years of experience playing video games. Not only was I a great pilot, I could also take out bogeys should we get attacked. Turns out it's far more complicated to fly the real ones.

One time on a flight from Columbus to Pittsburg, we did several barrel rolls in a row. If you pitch the nose of the plane up just before rolling it, you won't lose altitude. This is important because if you lose too much altitude, you get a radio call from the traffic control tower. Apparently, they think something is wrong when you suddenly drop hundreds of feet.

But I'll never forget the night Pete called and invited me on a short flight to Detroit and back. I figured this was another opportunity for me to hone my pilot skills. Forty minutes later I hopped in the right seat of another puddle jumper while he performed the pre-flight check. Flaps, check. Ailerons, check. Fuel, check. Everything was good so we made our way into the dark starry night with only the intermittent glowing lights from towns below.

I always loved flying at night. You kind of feel like you are from a different world than the little creatures moving around down below. As if you knew something they didn't know. As if you were living the life they wished they could live. You felt like you were on top of the world, literally.

But that feeling didn't last long. We flew directly into a storm. A colossal thunderstorm to be exact. My brother saw it on the radar and talked with command center or whoever it is pilots talk to through their headsets. They instructed us to climb to a different altitude to fly over the storm. We tried but didn't quite clear it. Rain began pelting the plane which sounded more like we were flying through hail. Wind tossed our little plane around like it was a tin can tied to the limo of a newly married getaway vehicle.

This wasn't just turbulence. It felt like we had angered the goddess of wind, and she was trying to knock us out of the sky.

Every few seconds, lightning would streak across the black sky and illuminate the rain. Lightning looks different when you are 10,000 feet in the air. In a nervous voice, I asked Pete if lightning ever struck airplanes while in the air.

"Yeah, sometimes, but most of the time it's not fatal," he said.

Most of the time! That wasn't very reassuring. In that moment, I realized just how small we were. I also realized that we were not in control. The wind was.

I feel like I can somewhat appreciate what Peter and the other eleven disciples might have felt inside the boat that night. They were not in control. The wind and the waves were. And if that wasn't bad enough, they saw a ghost walking toward them on the water. I don't know what I would have done in that prop airplane if lightning illuminated a figure floating toward us. No doubt I would have gotten closer to Jesus one way or another.

But Peter's experience with the wind goes to a different level the moment he decides to take a step *outside* of the boat. No longer can he use the boat to shield most of the wind. Now he feels the full force of its power beating against him. Not only is he trying something impossible, walking on water, but he's attempting it under the most intense conditions.

What I'm trying to say is the moment you decide to put your vision or dream out in the open, expect to feel the full force of the wind. That's not hyperbole talking, it's my personal experience.

Launching a capital campaign is one of the most dreaded parts of leading a church. I think some people have this mental picture of greedy pastors trying to pad the coffers when they ask people to give more money so they can build or expand facilities. Unfortunately, some unsavory televangelists have ruined it for the rest of us. Trust me, as someone who has led multiple capital campaigns over the years, it's really the last thing I want to do. Not only does a building project make your life way more complicated; it also puts your ministry and reputation at risk.

In 2016, I invited our church to give sacrificially so we could build a new facility. The vision was never just a bigger facility, but a place that would help us reach thousands for Christ and give away millions of dollars to help our city. My vision was always about creating space for people who were far from God to find hope, purpose, and a community they could belong to.

Some people think spending money on church facilities is a waste of resources. I've been told the church should only be using money to care for the poor and underprivileged. We had people leave our church shortly after we started the campaign. To them it just seemed like a waste of money that could help people in need. Of course, that's exactly what Judas said to Jesus when a woman "wasted" an entire bottle of fragrance on him. I'm not quite sure why we have to create a false dichotomy between helping the poor and building a physical place to meet spiritual needs. I believe the church should be doing both. I also firmly believe the more our community grows, the more resources we can gather to impact our city for good. It's the same as the old "the chicken or the egg" argument.

Our church responded in a huge way. It's an overwhelming feeling when people believe so much in your vision, they put their money toward it. We felt the wind of momentum at our back. Things were beginning to happen. It felt like God had put His hand on our plans.

By late 2016, our plans were moving faster than expected. We sold our Lithopolis building to someone in the church who let us stay and pay rent. *The Solomon Foundation* had approved our construction loan. We had money in the bank, pledges from a campaign, funding for the project, and zero debt. By the end of the year, we were given the green light to start moving dirt on our property.

More wind at our backs.

It was like God was guiding our every move.

Thanks for the push, God.

As we turned our calendars to 2017, the skies grew dark, and we heard the rumble of lightning in the distance. Windmills began to spin like scenes from the movie, *Twister*. A storm was coming, and we had no idea what was about to happen.

The city staff contacted us and said we had a problem. A FEMA problem. That's an acronym you don't want to hear mentioned when you have a major construction project underway. All work on the site came to a crashing halt. I never imagined learning so much about bridge engineering, hydraulics, modeling, and a bunch of other really expensive words.

For the next eighteen months, we were stuck in the middle of the sea buffeted by the wind and the waves. What we experienced wasn't just some difficult engineering hurdle; it was gale force wind coming at us from all sides. Like Peter, we were fully outside of the boat, and we felt it.

I'm not quite sure how to describe all the opposition we faced. All I can say is those were some of the worst years of my life. Everything fell apart — including me. My hopes and dreams for our church and my ministry were taking on water. My soul felt like it was drowning.

The project stalled and costs were mounting. We spent tens of thousands of dollars trying to find an engineering solution. During this time, I went on a short ministry break and came back to what can only be described as spiritual mutiny. We had to part ways with multiple staff members over the next year.

In February 2018, an anonymous email was sent to more than a hundred of our leaders claiming a pastor on our staff had acted inappropriately and our staff culture was toxic. I immediately asked our Board of Directors to do a full investigation into the allegations. We were all shocked to find out some of the claims were founded. It had happened right under my nose, and I was oblivious. I had to let that pastor go after being in ministry for nearly ten years together. It was gut-wrenching and the hardest thing I've had to do in ministry.

A couple of hundred people left the church in the midst of this drama. One of the people who left shared with me a "word from God" she received while reading a passage of Scripture calling out false, lying prophets. But then she gave me a hug when she was finished, so I guess it was done in "love." I've faced personal attacks, ministry attacks, and nearly had a nervous breakdown.

Opposition was knocking at my door.

I shouldn't have been surprised by this, yet I was. Every time we have attempted to take ground for God's kingdom, we have faced opposition. For example, when we were putting our plans in motion to start our church in 2003, my wife, Lorelei, got very sick. She couldn't eat without having excruciating abdominal pain. Her physician couldn't figure out what was causing it. She had become so weak and frail that she rarely got out of bed. When she weighed in at ninety-three pounds, we started to panic. Eventually, we found another doctor who discovered she had Crohn's Disease. With some different medications and a lot of prayer, it went into remission. We looked back on that moment and drew a connection between the launch of our church and her Crohn's Disease.

You'll never guess what happened when our small church took that huge step of faith to buy the property in Lithopolis just five years later. Lorelei's Crohn's came back with a vengeance. Coincidence or pattern? I began to see a correlation. Whenever we stepped out in faith, we faced serious opposition.

Now, here we were years later doing the same thing with this new building project in Canal Winchester. It was by far the biggest step of faith I've ever taken while pastoring our church. Thankfully, my wife's disease did not flare up. Instead, we faced opposition on every other front imaginable. Perhaps our spiritual enemy evolves.

I'm not telling you this to scare you, but to prepare you. Opposition will come. Expect it. I imagine that some of you reading this now may have already given up on a dream because you faced opposition. Maybe you were tempted to think you missed God completely because you faced spiritual headwind.

Perhaps we need to dump this idea that if God is "in something" we'll glide on smooth seas with His wind at our back.

OPPOSITION WILL COME. *EXPECT* IT.

It's so easy to reimagine the story of Israel receiving the Promised Land as if the previous tenants just packed up and left before they arrived. Who knows, maybe they even left small chocolates on the pillows and freshly washed towels in the bathrooms. Can I just remind you that is not how it happened?

The Israelites had to face giants, fortified cities, and nations with larger armies. They crossed over the Jordan River under Joshua's command expecting to face the hardest battles of their lives. Though God was leading them to their Promised Land, they still had to take possession of it with great opposition. And that generation of men had only seen small conflicts. They had spent most of their time grazing in the desert trying to survive in the wilderness.

We also should not be surprised when we face great opposition trying to advance God's Kingdom and expand His territory. Inhabitants don't like to be dispossessed. Just to be clear, we didn't forcefully take over any properties. We purchased everything legally. However, you can hold a physical deed to a parcel of land while the devil holds the spiritual deed to it.

You see, the Church is entrenched in an extraterrestrial battle between God and His spiritual enemy, Satan. Our mission is to expand God's Kingdom here on earth. To do that means we must take ground back from His archnemesis. Perhaps you would think it should be the other way around. We think the devil should be trying his best to take land back from the Creator. Surely, God holds the spiritual deed to everything we see, right?

Perhaps, but if that's the case, then why does Satan make Jesus a real estate offer when He was wandering in the wilderness for forty days and nights after His baptism? Let me remind you what the devil was offering with his sales contract.

Then the devil took him up and revealed to him all the kingdoms of the world in a moment of time. "I will give you the glory of these kingdoms and authority over them," the devil said, "*because they are mine to give to anyone I please*. I will give it all to you if you will worship me."

[Luke 4:5-7 NLT emphasis mine]

The price of this contract was Jesus falling down to worship the devil. Perhaps worship is the most expensive commodity in the spiritual realm. In exchange for Jesus' worship, He would receive the glory and *authority* over all the kingdoms of this world. Oh, and did you notice the fine print at the bottom of the sales contract? The devil could offer this in the contract because he said they are "mine to give to anyone I please."

That line has always given me pause and a lot of questions.

When did the authority of the kingdoms of this world get transferred over to the devil?

When God expelled Satan and his angels from heaven and sent them to earth, did he give them authority over it, or did they just claim squatters' rights?

If I recall, God originally gave *mankind* dominion over the earth.

> God blessed them and said to them, "Be
> fruitful and increase in number; *fill the*
> *earth* and *subdue* it. *Rule over* the fish in the
> sea and the birds in the sky and over every
> living creature that moves on the ground."
> [Genesis 1:28 emphasis mine]

It sure seems like God gave us the deed to earth. So, what happened? Perhaps something significant happened when Adam and Eve obeyed the authority of Satan over the authority of God. Perhaps in that early sinful exchange, we signed the deed over to the next landlord, Satan.

All I know is whenever we try to stake claim on a new piece of property here on earth, it is always a sign of aggression toward our enemy. Buying the land wasn't a sign of aggression; building on it was. Any time you choose to step out in faith and claim new ground for God, whether in ministry as a church or to expand God's Kingdom at your workplace or school, you are declaring war.

Expect a fight.

That is surely the lesson Peter learned as he stepped over the edge of the boat and immediately felt the violent wind keeping him from reaching Jesus. This was just the first of many fights he would face when trying to follow Jesus. When Peter preached about Jesus in the book of Acts, he faced intense opposition. He was thrown in prison, beaten, and threatened with execution if he continued to talk about Jesus. Of course, Peter never stopped. But I also have a sneaky suspicion that Peter knew his

ALWAYS LOOK FOR THE LION.

struggle was actually spiritual. He would later pen these words: "Stay alert! Watch out for your great enemy, the devil. He prowls around like a *roaring lion*, looking for someone to devour" (1 Peter 5:8 NLT emphasis mine).

Always look for the lion.

I'm not the kind of person that blames every hardship on the devil. I think we give him way too much credit. He's not omniscient (all-knowing), omnipotent (all-powerful), or omnipresent (all-present) like God. He surely isn't causing tires to go flat, alarm clocks to reset, or speed traps on the freeway. Although I do wonder if state troopers work for the devil. (No offense if you are a trooper.) I've just never met one that understood grace or mercy.

But I do believe there are times when we face significant attacks from our spiritual enemy to hinder us from fulfilling God's purpose and plan. The devil won't lie down and let you walk all over him. I wouldn't be surprised if we face Satan's elite special forces whenever we attempt to take territory for God's Kingdom.

I should have known the moment we bought land to establish a work of God in Canal Winchester we were setting ourselves up for war. Our church is relatively young. Old enough to vote, but not old enough to drink. When I drive to downtown Columbus and see one hundred-year-old beautiful church cathedrals, I am struck by the importance of owning property.

Those churches have lasted long after their founding leaders. It is a gentle reminder that the church I lead does not belong to me. I'm just stewarding my time and energy to gain whatever ground I can for God's Kingdom. Every time we see a majestic older church building, it should remind us God's Kingdom is firmly staked on that corner, regardless of the style of worship or denomination of the people in it. No matter how dark our culture gets, there is a beacon of light that will remain. God holds the deed to that parcel.

We tend to think in such short intervals, though, don't we? We think about raising our kids to eighteen and then releasing them to the wild (that is unless they boomerang back). We think about working forty years and then retiring. We think being married for twenty-five years is a long time. Perhaps it is for our current culture. We think about living for eighty or maybe even ninety years before we die.

We only think this way because of our finite limitations. We think this way because this is how we've experienced the world around us.

But neither God nor his eternally created nemesis, Satan, thinks this way. They are not bound by time like we are on earth. They are just bound in this timeless war over God's creation. They are fighting over you and me.

No one knew this better than the Apostle Paul. His ministry was traveling to new places to stake ground for God's Kingdom. On one particular trip, he landed in Ephesus, a port city on the west coast of modern-day Turkey. Paul began to share the Gospel first in the synagogues and then in the streets. Many heard the good news of Jesus and became Christians. Paul was so excited about the progress he ended up staying in Ephesus longer than he originally anticipated. He wrote these words in 1 Corinthians 16:

> But I will stay on at Ephesus until
> Pentecost, because a great *door* for effective
> work has *opened* to me, and there are many
> who *oppose* me.
>
> [1 Corinthians 16:8-9 emphasis mine]

In this one passage, Paul puts the final nail in the coffin of our wishful thinking that open doors mean smooth sailing. I love the juxtaposition Paul creates with the open door and many who oppose him. The truth is you will always find both!

OPEN DOORS LEAD TO OPPOSING FORCES.

Open doors lead to opposing forces.

This should put to bed the notion that if God is in *it,* we won't face opposition. In fact, if what you set out to do is *for* God, you better expect *many* who will oppose you. Opposition is always waiting on the other side of that unlocked door. The devil will never lie down and let you advance your God-given dream, purpose, or calling without a fight.

There's a lion waiting on the other side of that door.

Do you still want to walk through it?

> Then Peter got down out of the boat,
> walked on the water and came toward
> Jesus. But when he saw the wind, he was
> afraid and, beginning to sink, cried out,
> "Lord, save me!"
>
> [Matthew 14:29b-30]

Matthew uses an interesting choice of words when describing what happened to Peter. Of course, his vantage point was peering at Peter's backside over the edge of the boat. He didn't get to see his face or his reaction to the wind. But maybe Matthew could tell that Peter was no longer looking at Jesus by how his head darted back and forth in every direction. The truth is you can't really see wind; you can only see or feel the *effects* of it. Peter saw the wind rocking the boat sideways. He saw the rough whitecaps in the middle of the lake. He saw enough to distract him from keeping his eyes fixed on Jesus.

I have found that opposition will often distract us from the One who called us in the first place. Peter looked at the wind and waves and began to sink. It's when we take our eyes off Jesus and focus on what is coming against us that fear begins to fill our soul. Fear is a weight that affects our buoyancy. It was fear that caused Peter to sink.

I bet it was more than just his body that began to sink. His faith began to sink. His confidence began to sink. His courage began to sink.

I wonder what in you has begun to sink.

Have you lost hope that God will come through for you?

Have you begun to doubt your calling? Has the pain of moving toward your purpose caused you to shrink back?

Has the fear of failing, again, caused you to retreat?

Have you faced such painful headwind that you have all but given up?

If so, you might be convinced you did something wrong, and that God is no longer blessing you. Perhaps even now you are questioning if God is still with you. As the opposition gets fiercer, you've become less certain you heard God's voice in the first place. For those of you wondering how I can accurately describe your sinking soul, it's because I've experienced all of this.

In the end you have to decide what is louder — the voice that called you onto the waves or the howl of the wind coming against you. Because if you take your eyes off the One who called you, your faith will begin to sink. You'll question why you even got out of the boat in the first place. You'll start thinking to yourself, "the water is no place for me."

What I hope you see is that every scary step Peter took on the water brought him closer to Jesus and further from safety. The two go hand-in-hand.

We cannot live in safety and follow Jesus at the same time.

Unfortunately, our Western version of Christianity convinces us that following Jesus and living safely inside the boat can coalesce. That somehow a life with Christ is also a safe life. That's because most of us invite Jesus into our life rather than leaving our old life behind to follow Him. We try to add Jesus to our goals, dreams, and plans rather than surrendering them to Him. It would be like Peter trying to keep his fishing business and follow Jesus. Both Peter and the Apostle Paul knew differently.

Try to absorb Paul's words as you contemplate life in the boat or out on the water.

> I have been crucified with Christ and I no
> longer live, but Christ lives in me. The life I
> now live in the body, I live by faith in the
> Son of God, who loved me and gave himself
> for me.
>
> [Galatians 2:20]

Perhaps it's impossible to truly walk by faith *and* remain in the boat. Maybe the reason Jesus told Peter just two chapters later (Matthew 16) that he would hold the keys of the kingdom and be the first leader of the Church is because he was the only one with enough faith to get out of the boat. I can't help but wonder if Peter's willingness to risk drowning was all Jesus needed to know who should get the keys. Could it be a little shortsighted to look at Peter's sinking moment and think it was a dismal failure?

What if this was the moment that made Jesus crack a smile out the left side of His mouth and utter under His breath — he's the one!

8

WHEN THE GAP GETS BIGGER

"Every great move forward in your life begins with a leap of faith, a step into the unknown."

~ Brian Tracy

T HE UNITED STATES HATES to lose. Never was this more evident than in the Space Race in the 1960s. America and the Soviet Union had been engaged in a geopolitical Cold War for the previous two decades, the kind of war not fought on the battlefield but in a laboratory.

The United States and the Soviet Union were both threatening nuclear capability, and the race was on for supreme world dominance. It's kind of funny looking back. The US and Soviet Union were both acting like kids on the playground fighting for who gets the swings.

Like a male ostrich displaying its full plume for others to see, the Soviet Union displayed its technological prowess by launching Sputnik 1 on October 4, 1957. This was the first artificial satellite put into orbit around the earth. It caused fear and panic for the United States, as this gave the Soviet Union the high ground for any potential nuclear attack. Not to be outdone, President Dwight Eisenhower launched a program called National Aeronautics and Space Aviation (NASA), with the goal of putting a man into space.

As the United States was preparing to launch the first human into outer space, the Soviet Union beat them to the punch. On April 12, 1961, the Soviet Union bested the United States by twenty-four days when Yuri Gagarin launched into orbit around the globe. The US followed suit on May 5, 1961, when Alan Shepherd became the first American in outer space.

Of course, you can only imagine what coming in second did to the ego of the United States. So, President John F. Kennedy made a bold and public prediction just twenty-four days later (that can't be a coincidence). He declared that before the decade was up, the United States would put a man on the moon and bring him back safely to earth.

Sure enough, on July 20, 1969, the entire world watched as Neil Armstrong descended the ladder of Apollo 11 onto the moon, took his first step onto the moon's surface and uttered these famous words –

"That's one small step for man, one giant leap for mankind."

(Neil Armstrong)

I can't think of a better description of what it feels like to take a step of faith for God.

Whether you are stepping onto the water or onto the moon, it's the unknown that defines a step of faith. Walking by faith is going where God calls you even if no one has gone that way before. And every mission you take by faith will surely be met with challenges that might turn even the smallest step into a giant leap.

There were several things that jeopardized the mission of Apollo 11. Previous training attempts prior to takeoff ended in disasters that nearly killed the crew. While on the mission, the crew ran into several problems while preparing to land on the moon. These delays also caused them to run low on fuel. I can live with running my car on empty, but I'm not so sure I'd trust the lunar capsule to work the same way.

The crew missed the window for the intended landing zone on the moon and had to divert last minute to avoid boulders and craters that would have destroyed them. Even worse, they accidentally broke a switch needed to launch them back off the moon. That would seem kind of important. Oh, and bad weather threatened their safe return to earth.

What often starts out as a small step of faith can quickly turn into a massive leap of faith. Your baby steps might turn into lunar missions. For whatever reason, it seems like God enjoys stretching our steps into leaps. The question is, how will you respond when the gap of faith gets bigger?

Four thousand five hundred years before we landed on the moon, God used outer space to teach Abraham about the gap of faith.

Abraham (also known as Abram) is a legendary figure when it comes to faith. He is considered the founding father of three of the world's largest religions– Judaism, Islam, and Christianity. In both the Old and New Testaments, Abraham's name is synonymous with faith. But even Abraham had his share of doubts. Before he became a legend, he took a single step.

In Genesis 12, God spoke to Abraham and called him to move to a distant land. God didn't give him the exact coordinates either. He just told Abraham to move in faith and God would show him the spot when he arrived.

I love the way the writer of Hebrews describes this act of faith.

> By faith Abraham, when called to go to a
> place he would later receive as his
> inheritance, obeyed and went, even though
> he did not know where he was going.
> [Hebrews 11:8]

That's faith.

Walking without a waypoint.

Moving without all the information.

Stepping without knowing.

The one thing that gave Abraham the courage to move was the promise God gave him. In return for his obedience, God promised to make Abraham a father of many nations. Not only was moving his family an act of faith but believing God for a son was also an act of faith.

When God spoke to Abraham in Genesis 12, he was seventy-five and his wife, Sarah, was sixty-five. They had tried to have children unsuccessfully for decades. There were no fertility clinics back in those days, no medical procedures to help in these situations. So, you can imagine what it must have been like for Abraham to hear God promise to make him a dad.

Nevertheless, Abraham was obedient to God and moved with his wife and nephew. However, with every flip of the calendar year, it seemed God wasn't holding up His end of the deal. About ten years passed by and still no pregnancy.

One night, God appeared to Abraham in a vision with these words.

> "Do not be afraid, Abram.
> I am your shield,
> your very great reward."

WHEN THE GAP GETS BIGGER

[Genesis 15:1b]

Abraham wasn't really in the mood to hear more of what seemed like empty promises. You can tell by his snarky response back to God.

> But Abram said, "Sovereign Lord, what can you give me since I remain childless and the one who will inherit my estate is Eliezer of Damascus?" And Abram said, "You have given me no children; so, a servant in my household will be my heir."
>
> [Genesis 15:2-3]

You get the feeling Abraham is a bit discouraged. He took a step of faith and the gap got bigger. It's quite unheard of for a woman to have children at sixty-five years old, but it seems absolutely impossible at seventy-five. That's how old Sarah was and, let's face it, Abraham was no spring chicken at eighty-five. He had resigned to giving his estate to his chief servant, Eliezer.

Perhaps you've been there. You've taken a step for God, but instead of your foot landing on the promise, it only opened up into an even bigger step, or maybe a nearly impossible leap.

The moment you moved forward in faith, the goalpost moved further away.

The moment you started your business, you received a major setback with your first and only client.

The moment you told people what you felt called to do, they said you were making the biggest mistake of your life.

The moment you quit your job, the funding you were depending on was jerked out from under you like a rug.

I know this feeling all too well. When we moved forward with building a new facility in 2016, it was already a massive step of faith. Just to give you some perspective, our rent payment was going to increase by 800 percent. We had positioned ourselves well in regard to saving money and having no debt, but this new project was going to push us to the brink of failure. I couldn't tell if it was faith or stupidity. God continued to open doors and we continued to walk through them.

When the city stopped our progress in January 2017, it cost us far more than just time. At that moment, our economy was booming and the need for construction services was at an all-time high. There was a nationwide shortage of materials and skilled labor. This was driving the cost of construction up *monthly!* All of that, combined with the setbacks of dealing with FEMA and other civil engineering issues, and before you know it, our project was delayed for nearly two years.

By the time we finally worked through all the problems with site development, our general contractor had to renew his quote. Without changing a single design on the project, the cost for building our new facility increased more than 2.5 million dollars!

Yes, let that sink in.

Our rent just climbed to ten times what we were currently paying.

Well, I thought, I'm done!

Not only was the cost of the project soaring, but our support was shrinking. In the previous chapter, I shared some of the drama we faced within the church. I was forced to make very difficult leadership decisions that prompted hundreds of people to leave. I knew they were the right decisions to make, but that didn't make it feel any better. Over those two years, all I can say is the gap got much bigger.

Even bigger than my faith.

Finally, after eighteen months of hearing *No*, the city finally said *Go*. I couldn't believe it! We jumped every engineering hurdle, removed all the roadblocks, and cut through every inch of red tape. I honestly thought this day would never come. And while everyone was congratulating me like I just completed my first marathon, fear had taken up residence in me. Though given the green light to move forward, everything inside of me was yelling "stop!" I was discouraged, confused and, to be honest, frustrated with God.

My thoughts began to betray me.

"I'm doing all this for You, God.

I wasn't sure we could afford this in the first place, now it seems impossible.

What am I going to do?

Maybe I should just pack up and move somewhere warmer."

In that moment, I think I knew a little of how Abraham felt. I didn't want to hear how God was my protector and my great reward. I was convinced God had forgotten about me. What was already a stretch was now an impossibility. Maybe not for God, but it was for our church.

That's when God told Abraham to take another step — a step outside.

Then the Lord took Abram outside and said
to him, "Look up into the sky and count the
stars if you can. That's how many
descendants you will have!"

[Genesis 15:5 NLT]

I love this. God took Abraham outside. God couldn't get
Abraham to see what he needed to see *inside* his tent. Far too often
we place our man-made limitations on what God can do. Yes,

LOOK UP INTO THE SKY AND COUNT THE *STARS* IF YOU CAN.

Abraham and Sarah were ten years
older, but that didn't make God any
less capable of giving them a son. The
problem comes when our limited faith
takes the place of God's limitless
power.

God took Abraham outside
and told him to do two things.

Look up into the sky and count the stars if you can.

I live about twenty-five miles southeast of Columbus,
Ohio. The sky near my house looks quite different than in the city.
If you live in or near a city, I encourage you to take a drive one

evening this week to a remote place away from light pollution and look up. Let your eyes gaze on the twinkling lights of the vast cosmos.

The number of stars you can see with your naked eye depends on how dark the backdrop is. Abraham was camping in the middle of nowhere when God told him to look up and count the stars. Let's just say it was going to take Abraham a while to try.

While on the surface, this might seem like nothing more than a good sermon illustration, some further exploration might be helpful to our faith. So exactly how many stars can we count on any given night? Any guesses? Rather than attempt that on my own, I will lean on someone who has already done that.

Astronomer Dorrit Hoffleit from Yale University has actually counted all the stars visible to us from Earth. She compiled a catalog from her work of counting every star visible with 6.5 magnification – the limit of the human eye. If you put all the visible stars on the earth from both hemispheres on the darkest of nights, you can count 9,096 stars. But since we can only be in one hemisphere at a time, we can naturally only see about 4,500 stars. I'm trying to picture Abraham lying on his back with his pointer finger in the air.

1...2...3...4...5...6... wait, did I count that one already? I wonder how many times he had to start over. Okay, he probably never even tried.

"Okay, God, I get the point," Abraham must have thought.

But if we stop there, we might miss a deeper revelation. Maybe it's what we *can't* see that should build our faith even more. God didn't just tell Abraham to count the stars if he can, God also told Abraham to *look into the sky*. Perhaps there is more than what we can see with our own eyes.

If you used a good pair of 50mm binoculars on the highest magnification, you could possibly see as many as 217,000 stars. If you switched over to a 3-inch telescope, the night sky would offer up more than 5.3 million stars.1

But that's not all. What else do you see when you look up into the night sky? I'm not talking about the stars or even the moon. Do you see anything else? What about the *gaps* surrounding the stars?

If your answer is, *nothing, it's all black*, then God might whisper — look again.

In the twentieth century, astronomers and astrophysicists had to take another look at the black void of our starry night skies.

What we originally thought was just empty space for thousands of years is now thought to be filled with *dark matter*. Scientists have come to this conclusion not because of what they have observed, but the observable effects of what they can't see. I find it a bit ironic that our scientific community has reached a conclusion based on something they can't see or measure. (Shhh... Don't tell them, but that sounds a lot like faith!)

This was discovered because the speed at which things move in space doesn't fit within the parameters of our universal constants. If objects are traveling aimless in space, the only thing that should be affecting their velocity is gravity. However, the observed variations don't add up to *just* gravitational calculations. Something else is slowing down the movement of objects in space. We now associate this with *dark matter*. (Hang with me, we are going somewhere with this.) Though we have no idea what it is or how to measure it, we know it's there because it affects *what* we can measure. In fact, most scientists have collectively accepted that we only know about five percent of all matter or energy that exists in our universe. The other ninety-five percent is made up of matter and energy that does not reflect, absorb, or emit light.2

It's there, even if we can't see it.

If that doesn't expand your view of God, I don't know what will. When God told Abraham to look up into the night sky,

He was pointing to more than just stars. God was showing off the things He has created that we can't see too! The next time you gaze at a night sky littered with starry lights, remember who made the *gap* surrounding the stars.

Perhaps this is God's way of saying, "You can trust me even when the gap gets bigger — because I made the gap too." You could say He's the *God of the Gaps*.

Why does this matter? Because if you are going to operate in the realm of faith you better get used to trusting God with all that you can't see. You might even have to accept that God may delay the vision, allow the project costs to soar, shrink your support base, and drive you to your knees in submission before you move any further. It's not just about what God wants to do *through* you, it's also about what God wants to do *in* you.

HE'S THE GOD OF THE GAPS

I think God likes it when the odds are stacked against Him. That's not conjecture; it's what you see in many of the miracles God performs throughout the Bible. It's never more apparent than in the story of Gideon.

In Judges 6, we discover the Israelites are living under constant oppression from the Midianites. God removed His protection because they were worshiping false gods. Eventually, they turned back to God for help, and He answered by tapping Gideon on the shoulder.

Gideon was a nobody who was hiding from the Midianites when God called him to rescue the Israelites. At least that is how Gideon saw himself. Honestly, I can relate to Gideon a lot. I didn't have any great skill or training when God called me to serve Him in full-time ministry. Maybe that's how you feel about yourself. If so, I've got good news for you. God specializes in using ordinary people to do extraordinary things.

> Then the Lord turned to him and said, "Go
> with the strength you have, and rescue Israel
> from the Midianites. I am sending you!"
> [Judges 6:14 NLT]

Gideon was quite shocked when God asked him to save the nation of Israel using his own strength. He came from the smallest tribe of Israel and was the least in his family. Gideon was pretty sure God had the wrong address and, certainly, the wrong person.

Finally, God convinced Gideon to take charge of the situation. He mustered as many troops as he could to face an army so numerous even their camels were like the grains of the sand and couldn't be counted (Judges 7:12). Gideon assembled 32,000 men to fight for Israel. These were terrible odds for Gideon as the Midian army had more than 120,000 warriors ready for battle.

But God thought those odds were still too high for Gideon.

> The Lord said to Gideon, "You have *too many* warriors with you. If I let all of you fight the Midianites, the Israelites will boast to me that they saved themselves by their own strength. Therefore, tell the people, 'Whoever is timid or afraid may leave this mountain and go home.'" So, 22,000 of them went home, leaving only 10,000 who were willing to fight.
>
> [Judges 7:2-3 NLT emphasis mine]

God didn't like 4:1 odds in favor of the Midianites. Remember, God likes to stack the odds against Himself. So, God proceeded to shrink the size of Gideon's army from 32,000 down to 10,000 men. Now the odds are 12:1 in favor of Midian. I'm sure Gideon was probably freaking out about now.

But God still wasn't done.

> The Lord told Gideon, "There are *still* too many!
>
> [Judges 7:4a NLT emphasis mine]

Really God?

God had Gideon reduce the army to just 300 men. My guess is they didn't even look like the actors who played in the movie *300*. If I'm doing my math right, that's 400:1 odds in favor of Gideon's enemy. I can picture Gideon standing there trying to do quick math in his head thinking all we need is for each one of our men to kill 400 of theirs and we can win this. Let's just say what was already a huge step of faith for Gideon just became an insurmountable jump across the Grand Canyon on a tricycle.

Although I didn't have more than 120,000 soldiers wanting to kill me, I can still relate. When we started our building project, it was already stretching my faith. Now, it seemed like the gap had become insurmountable.

I was sitting in my office when I received the updated price quote for the construction project. When I opened the email and read the quote, I thought, *the project is dead.* There was no way we could move forward like this. It was a stretch before, but now it seemed impossible. It felt like the odds for this project had gone from 4:1 to 100:1 from just that one email.

My mind raced as I thought about all the people who had given sacrificially for two years toward this vision. Now it wasn't going to happen. We had just come off one of the most painful seasons as a church and to deliver this bad news might just be the terms of my resignation. I wanted to run away for good. I think I might have even looked for a house in Florida that day.

I grabbed my phone and called Doug Crozier, the CEO of *The Solomon Foundation.* I told him the new price tag, fully expecting him to shut the project down. I figured at least I could tell our church that our funding was revoked. At least then they might go easy on me when they flogged me. What he said to me took me by surprise.

"If you don't build now, you never will," he said.

I calmly stated, "I don't have another 2.5 million dollars."

Doug assured me they would be in our corner and would help us get it built. It was nice to know they would lend us more money, but I still had no idea how we would be able to pay for it. I hung up the phone and thought, well that didn't bail me out. Now what?

So, I called my Board of Directors and told them all the new information about the project and what Doug had said. In separate conversations, all of them agreed we needed to move forward and build.

C'mon guys, you aren't helping me out here.

I then called a good friend and mentor of mine, Tim Liston. I was lamenting about our situation and told him I didn't know what to do. The question he asked me that day has stuck with me ever since.

"What did you feel God called you to do before all of this happened?" he asked.

"Build it," I replied.

In a gentle, leading voice he said, "Then that's your answer. You can't let money keep you from doing what you feel God called you to do. If God called you to build it, you have to trust Him to provide."

I'd like to say I got off the phone and told our team we were moving forward right then. But I didn't. I continued to wrestle with this huge life-altering, ministry-defining decision. This may bankrupt our church. I'd given fifteen years of my life building this church and I could lose it all. This one decision could define the rest of my life. I wrestled and prayed and fasted until there was no other option available. Finally, I yielded to my faith and told fear to shut up.

The church gave a standing ovation when I told them the news. We green-lighted the project and within months we held a groundbreaking ceremony. We were all in.

Then COVID happened.

Really God?

The gap has never been bigger.

I could picture God sitting on His throne with a slight grin on His face saying, "I like these odds."

9

THE WEIGHT OF FAITH

"No one knows the weight of another's burden."
~ George Herbert

I'M NOT SURE IF any movie has ever been quoted more than *Jerry Maguire*. This 1996 box office smash has given us epic lines such as, "show me the money," and "you had me at hello." Of course, most women probably remember the moment when heartthrob Tom Cruise (Jerry Maguire) says to Renee Zellweger (Dorothy Boyd) "you complete me." I wonder how many times that cheesy phrase has been used by lovesick boyfriends.

These quotes are permanently etched in the neocortex of my brain. But as famous as these lines are, there is one that rises above them all for me. It wasn't even originally written in the script. When the director heard six-year-old actor Jonathan Lipnicki (Ray Boyd) saying it to other actors on the set, he had it put in the movie.

In a scene where Dorothy's son, Ray, is challenging her new love interest (Jerry Maguire) with his knowledge, he blurts out...

Do you know the human head weighs eight pounds?

For some reason that useless fact has always stuck with me. Although I never want to know exactly how much my head weighs, as that would mean it would have to be detached from my body, I do believe some heads weigh more than others. I know that sounds rude, but hear me out.

It's obvious some people naturally have larger craniums than others. I have a small head and look quite funny in hats. There is clearly physical diversity within the human species.

What I am talking about is the weight of the dreams we carry *inside* our heads.

When I say dreams, I'm not talking about the kind we have with our eyes closed at night. You know, the one where your cat turns on you only to find out he's a Brazilian black belt in Jiu-Jutsu and you run for your life. Not that kind of dream. I'm talking about the kind of dream we see when our eyes are open. This is not the kind of dream that allows you to sleep peacefully. This kind of dream will keep you awake at night. It will fester in your soul until you do something about it. It feels like a burden.

It looks impossible.

It won't leave you alone.

It feels connected to your destiny.

It's been said dreaming with your eyes open means you are willing to see what others can't imagine. Visionaries dream with their eyes open. They see a better future and give their lives to building it. I believe God has a vision for each and every one of us to fulfill. That includes you!

I don't know if you have one of those dreams for your life, but I hope you do. Anything less is a lesser life than God created you for. God has put a divine echo inside us all. A longing for a world far better than the one we are in now. The problem is, many of us have learned how to shut it out. It *scares* us.

In America, many Christians spend more time chasing the American Dream than a God-given dream. We exchange our purpose for a paycheck — our calling for a career. We spend our days trying to build a life rather than using the life we have to build God's Kingdom. This might be the most tragic waste of the divine imprint placed solely on our species.

What separates humans from the rest of God's creation is the power to choose our future – both for the good or the bad.

WE EXCHANGE OUR PURPOSE FOR A PAYCHECK.

This is clear from the story of Adam and Eve in Genesis. God placed a man and woman in a tropical paradise and invited them to enjoy any of the lush grapes, delicious apples, ripe bananas, or sweet mangos in the garden, with only one exception. They were not to touch the tree in the middle of it. This tree was known as the Tree of the Knowledge of Good and Evil, and it came with great and terrible powers. God warned them that if they touched this tree, it would kill them.

Some have questioned why a good and loving God would even allow such a tree to exist. If God created everything, then it means He made *that* tree. If God loved mankind so much, wouldn't He have protected them from making the biggest mistake of their lives?

Great question.

What's the answer?

Love. Only when we understand true love can we begin to grasp why God would create such a tree in the first place.

God's love for us is evident in the world He created for us. God told the man and woman they can enjoy almost *everything* in the garden! Yet, the only way God could receive a pure, unprovoked, and authentic love response back from His creation was to give us the power to choose *not* to love Him. Only then would God be the recipient of that kind of love from us. Love that is forced or required is not truly love.

So, the all-powerful Creator put the power in our hands by asking us to not touch this one tree. This tree was the proverbial cookie jar on the counter. Although the pantry was full of Little Debbies, Twinkies, cake, doughnuts, and every other imaginable goodie, the man and woman couldn't take their eyes off the prohibited cookie jar. In the end, they put their hand in the jar, and we are still paying the consequences.

We must realize the weight of this divine gift. We have only one life. God has given us the gift of life and the power to choose what we do with it. Our most precious resource is not how much money we can make or the skills and talents we possess. It's *time*. It's the one commodity of which we never have enough and can't buy more.

You have the power to choose how you live every moment. You can spend your time, energy, and resources building *your* life or you can spend it building God's Kingdom here on earth. The power is in your hands.

Most people will spend their entire lives searching for meaning and purpose and never find it. That's because you will never find it while focused on yourself. But here's some good news. I'm convinced our purpose will find *us*.

How? It comes as that burden that won't leave us alone. It comes when we see what is wrong in this world and decide to be the one to do something about it. It comes through a dream that won't let us sleep.

And only those who *respond* to the dream inside of them begin to walk in their God-given purpose.

Seth and Tammy know what it means to have their purpose find them. They have been a part of our church for several years and served at some of our local outreach opportunities providing beds to families in need. One Sunday, when Seth was at church praying over prayer requests from our community, he kept getting interrupted with the thought that he was supposed to start a furniture bank. In fact, every time he closed his eyes to pray, he would picture a green building he had never seen before. Later that day, straight out of the blue, Tammy said to Seth, "I think we are supposed to start a furniture bank."

Their purpose found them.

Three days after having this dream dropped on him, Seth was driving to a job site when he spotted a green building out of the corner of his eye. It just so happened that this building was for sale. All the details fell into place for them to buy this building. Seeing this as a sign from God, they started *Compassion Furniture Bank*, a non-profit organization that gives

THEIR PURPOSE FOUND THEM.

away gently used furniture free of charge to families in need.

Sometime later, Tammy was running through the park with her sister when she came to an abrupt stop. She said God spoke to her and told her that the white box truck she was looking at parked in someone's driveway was going to belong to the furniture bank. Three weeks later, she stopped by that same house and caught the owner outside. She asked if he would be willing to sell it to them. Little did she know what had happened to him three weeks earlier. He told her he had been outside mowing his grass when the thought dropped into his mind, "I'm supposed to sell that truck and I don't know why."

Only God.

I hope with everything in me that God is lighting a match to the dry timber of your soul right now. Perhaps you once had a dream to serve the homeless or go on a mission trip or step into lay leadership or go back to school or leave the marketplace to be a stay-at-home mother, but you didn't have the faith to pursue it. Let me look right at you through the pages of this book and say — it's never too late to take the first step. Don't let regret keep you in the boat one second longer.

Today, decide to pursue that God-given dream, even if it means something as simple as writing it down on paper or telling someone what's in your heart. Don't waste another minute of your life without putting energy toward a new future. God is waiting for you to activate your faith for the dream He has put within you.

On August 28, 1963, more than 250,000 people marched on the streets of Washington DC for racial equality. Dr. Martin Luther King, Jr. gave the world a glimpse of the dream he carried with his famous "I have a dream" speech. This wasn't just a dream for himself. It was a dream for his daughters and every future generation. Dr. King's dream became a catalyst for a civil rights movement in America. That kind of dream is heavy. It's also costly.

Dr. King showed us what it means to give yourself for a higher purpose. His dream would eventually cost him his life when he was assassinated on April 4, 1968. Dr. King isn't the only one who shares this dream of racial equality. Millions of Americans also believe in this dream, too. But there is a line of demarcation that separates those who believe in a dream from those who risk it all to build the dream. Dr. King crossed that line, and we are forever grateful.

Only those who are willing to get out of the boat know the weight they carry once they're on the water. Our friend, Peter, who responded to Jesus' invitation to walk on the water probably felt fifty pounds heavier the moment his right foot hit the water's surface. Why? Peter was carrying the hope of the other eleven on his shoulders. No one else in the boat asked if they could risk drowning to walk on water. Peter stepped out of the boat alone, with twenty-four eyes (don't forget Jesus was there) fixed on him the entire time. There's a weight that comes with carrying the dream.

There's another famous guy from the Old Testament who knows the weight of carrying a dream. His name is Moses. Perhaps you've heard the story of God using this Hebrew deliverer to free the nation of Israel from oppressive slavery. Movies have been made about his story. Although we all love the idea of being the hero of a blockbuster hit, very few of us would want to be in Moses' shoes.

Let me paint the scene before you sign up for the casting call. Moses grew up in the lap of luxury in an Egyptian palace. You might say he literally grew up with a silver spoon in his mouth. Although Moses was of Hebrew descent, he was adopted and raised by the daughter of the Pharaoh. This afforded him special privileges like not being beaten regularly and forced into slave labor as was the fate for his fellow Israelites.

Moses' guilt finally caught up by the time he was forty years old. He just couldn't continue to turn a blind eye to the injustice his people faced daily. Perhaps this was the moment

Moses' dream of rescuing his fellow people was birthed. One day, he snapped and killed an Egyptian taskmaster for beating a Hebrew slave. Word of this got back to the Pharaoh, and Moses ran for his life.

For the next forty years, Moses lived a new life as a shepherd in the wilderness. He must have blocked the urge to rescue his people from his mind. He moved on, but God didn't. One day while tending sheep, God appeared to him through a burning bush. It was here that God called Moses back to that dream and back to Egypt to deliver the Israelites from their oppression.

If you know the story, then you are familiar with the ten miraculous plagues that God brought on the nation of Egypt. God finally broke the spirit of Pharaoh and he let all the Israelite slaves go free. You would think that would be the final scene — Moses rides off in a chariot holding his spear in the air while cinematic music cues the rolling credits. But that is hardly the end of the story or the dream.

You see, the dream God gave Moses was to reach the Promised Land. Leaving Egypt might have been the easiest part of the story for Moses. After all, God did all the heavy lifting in Egypt. Now, Moses had to carry the responsibility for upwards of two million people as they wandered into the death trap known as the Wilderness. It's here that Moses would really feel the weight of this God-given dream.

Deep in the desert, the people of God run out of food and water. In Numbers 11, Moses finds himself with nearly four million angry eyes fixed on him. The people begin to grumble and complain and wish they were back in Egypt where at least they had food to survive. Moses feels the weight of responsibility that comes with being the one carrying the dream and has an honest moment with God.

Listen to his complaint.

> And Moses said to the Lord, "Why are you treating me, your servant, so harshly? Have mercy on me! What did I do to deserve the burden of all these people? Did I give birth to them? Did I bring them into the world? Why did you tell me to carry them in my arms like a mother carries a nursing baby? How can I carry them to the land you swore to give their ancestors? Where am I supposed to get meat for all these people? They keep whining to me, saying, 'Give us meat to eat!' I can't carry all these people by

myself! The load is far *too heavy*! If this is
how you intend to treat me, just go ahead
and kill me. Do me a favor and spare me
this misery!"
[Numbers 11:11-15 NLT emphasis mine]

Notice what Moses said: "I can't carry all these people by myself. The load is far too heavy!" The thought of leading the people to the Promised Land was so weighty Moses opted for God to kill him on the spot. That's heavy.

Though you and I may never know what it's like to have millions of people look to us for deliverance like Dr. King and Moses did, that doesn't mean we won't feel the weight of stepping out of the boat with eyes on us. There is nothing more humbling than realizing God is calling you to lead other people to a better future. There is nothing scarier than realizing what happens if you fail.

Growing up as a PK, I knew all too well the weight of ministry. I had seen what my parents carried for many years and how heavy the burden of leadership is. However, when you are called to something, you can't escape it.

As I mentioned earlier, I tried, but my purpose found me. When I ran from God, I was also running from my purpose. But the moment I stopped running from God, my purpose caught up with me. From that "burning bush" moment in my early twenties, I knew ministry would be the only thing that fulfilled me. Once your purpose finds you, nothing else will satisfy.

What I never imagined was the weight I would carry to lead people in ministry. Nothing prepared me for it. When you realize that your influence and decisions will lead people to change the course of their lives or give sacrificially to your vision, it humbles you greatly. And when you step out in faith and risk everything for the sake of God's kingdom, you quickly discover just how much your decision weighs.

It never felt heavier than on April 1, 2019, which also happened to be my twelve-year anniversary of going into full-time ministry. After overcoming years of waiting and opposition, we were finally ready to pour the foundation of our new church facility. We gathered our staff and a few key leaders for this special moment. It literally felt like we were standing on holy ground. If the level of opposition was any indication of what God would do, we knew it was special.

Our staff gathered around massive holes dug for the footer just hours before the concrete trucks would fill them. We prayed and dedicated the moment to God as we poured hundreds of stones into the holes. Not just any stones, these stones had the names of people on them that our church was believing God would rescue for eternity. It was a holy and powerful moment for our staff. But for me, it was especially heavy.

If a human head weighs eight pounds, how much does an entire body weigh?

More than I wanted to know.

You see, we didn't just bury people's prayers in the foundation, we also buried a body. Before you call the FBI, let me explain.

Janice is one of my favorite human beings in the entire world. She and her husband, Israel, came to our church at the end of 2010. They fell in love with the vision and decided to make it their new church home. Everyone in our community fell in love with them, especially with Israel. He was the sweetest guy. He had a servant's heart and a thick Puerto Rican accent. I could always hear him talking back to me while I was preaching, saying things like, "Ah-min (amen) or Forgeeve (forgive) us Lord."

Janice joined our worship band to play keys and Israel came early with her every Sunday. Every week he served as a camera operator, which was funny since he had a medical condition that was causing him to go blind. He didn't care what we asked him to do; he just wanted to serve. We had to always remind him to keep his hands on the camera because he constantly took them off the controls to worship. He couldn't help himself. He was that in love with Jesus.

Just four years later, Israel had a massive brain hemorrhage that took his life at only fifty years old. He was so beloved by our community that we packed the church for his funeral, which felt more like a high-energy worship experience. His funeral is what I would want mine to be.

For Janice, Israel was a gift from heaven after the abusive first marriage she had suffered through. I watched Janice walk through those dark moments of grief with a deep trust in God. Her faith in the wake of all that she dealt with continues to inspire me. She, too, has a deep love for Jesus that convicts you every time you talk with her. Not long after Israel passed, an opportunity came for Janice to join our staff. She took it. It had been her dream to be on staff at our church and everything aligned for her to leave a career in the medical field and join our team.

What I didn't know leading up to that dedication day is that Janice still had Israel's ashes. She had spread some of them in Puerto Rico. But she kept most of them for *this* moment. As our staff finished praying over the stones, Janice pulled out a white cardboard box with the rest of Israel's ashes in it.

She told us that she knew Israel would want to be right here when this church was built because he believed in this vision so much. With not a dry eye in the place, Janice poured the rest of Israel's ashes into that foundation. As the ashes fell into the hole, a weight fell on me. I don't know how much a body weighs when it's ashes, but it felt like a ton that morning. I realized right then what was at stake.

This leap of faith I led our church to take wouldn't just affect me, it would affect all of us. It wasn't just the livelihoods of nearly two dozen staff members. It was also their lives. It was their dream, too. It was something we all sacrificed for. The thought of failing Janice with her husband's ashes immortalized in the foundation was overwhelming. Fear began to saturate my thoughts.

"What if this doesn't work and we lose the building?

What if the property is sold to a dealership or grocery store?

What if her husband is forever laid to rest under a Honda dealership?!"

Our minds create wild narratives under intense pressure. I kept a good face for the rest of the staff, but inside I was dying. It was like someone tied an anchor to my soul that day.

I have no idea how much faith weighs. If we could put it on the scale, I imagine it would be measured in metric tons. The bigger the dream, the more it will weigh. Even a dream that can change one person's future is considerable, but having a dream that can affect thousands will come at an unbelievable cost. Anytime you need others to help you reach a dream, it will be heavier. Anytime you have to put someone's future at risk to dare for the impossible, it adds tonnage to the scale.

I don't share this to scare you. I know this chapter might seem counterintuitive to my goal for writing this book. In the end, I hope this book pushes you out of the boat. But I also wish someone had prepared me for the weight I would carry to take these steps of faith. Thankfully, I have some incredible mentors in my life who have been coaching me and a counselor who has been a lifeline.

My good friend, Tim, pastors a large church in Houston, Texas. On any given weekend, his church has more than 10,000 people attending one of their many locations. His voice has been a life vest in the storm for me. I'm grateful to have a friend and mentor who has carried this kind of weight before. He could always calm me down with his words.

"You can do this. God's got this. It's time to put your big boy pants on and start leading."

Even though I'm not six years old, those words always pushed me to keep going.

Perhaps in the end, this is how we *build* faith. You see, everyone wants to be a person of great faith, but very few have considered what it takes to *get* real faith. Building faith is like building muscle. It won't happen overnight, and it takes a lot of reps before you see any progress. If you want stronger muscles, you put more weight on them. I've learned that lesson from years of working out at the gym.

Several years ago, before I tore my shoulder, I was trying to set a PR (personal record) on the bench press. After all, bench press is the only number guys care about. I was taking supplements and working out to build my chest twice each week. My bench press was growing rapidly because of some advice I had been given by a friend at the gym. He encouraged me to do *negatives* on the bench. I know some of you are just dying to know what a negative rep is on bench, so I'll tell you.

A negative rep is when you put more weight on the bar than you can normally press. With a spotter's help, you slowly lower the bar down to your chest, keeping as much resistance on it as you can. When the bar finally reaches your chest, your spotter helps pull the bar up and you do it again. There is something about getting your muscles used to the heavier weight that eventually enables you to push more.

To build faith, you must do the same. You will have to put yourself in the position where the bar weighs more than you can handle. Thankfully, you have a Supernatural Spotter who is all-powerful. Cheesy... I know. But it's true! This is the essence of faith. It's putting yourself in situations where God has to do the heavy lifting, even if you have to struggle under the weight of it.

Every step of faith I've taken has gotten successively bigger. New levels, new devils. I can hear the old preacher now. Each new step carries more risk and bigger stakes. And trust me, there is always another step. Sometimes following Jesus feels like being on a Stairmaster. There's always another step coming. But here's what I've discovered: even if the steps get bigger, so do my leg muscles. The need is greater, but so is my faith to believe God for it.

My hope is that today you will put a little more on the bar than you've had on it before. God wants to call you to a new PR in the gym of faith. Will you trust Him to be your spotter? Just know that He is doing it for your good and He won't let the bar crush you.

So, take a deep breath, grip the bar and lift.

HOW MUCH DOES A CLOUD WEIGH?

by Tim Moore

How much does a cloud weigh?

Is it as light as a feather?

Perhaps, even lighter.

Defying gravity.

Suspended far above.

Pushed by the wind.

So easy to shove.

Until the day it falls to the ground.

Its weight is easily measured by the pound.

Torrents and showers causing sea levels to grow.

For surely the skies weigh more than we know.

10

THE ANATOMY OF FEAR & FAITH

"The only thing we have to fear is fear itself."
~ *Franklin D. Roosevelt*

DID I MENTION THE time I almost broke off my engagement to my wife? We had a moment that nearly ended our twenty-five-year marriage before it began.

Lorelei wanted us to spend the day at Kings Island, an amusement park in Mason, Ohio. She loves theme parks, rides, and attractions. I do not. If I had known she would develop such an obsession with Disney, I might not have gone through with the wedding. But I'm stuck with her and Disney forever.

I know many of you are judging me right now. You're probably wondering what kind of person doesn't like theme parks or rides? Well, before you form any more unfair opinions of me, I should probably tell you about a traumatic experience I had when I was ten years old.

My parents took our family to Disneyland. I don't remember that day very well, as I have blocked it from my memory. But my parents told me what happened when we rode Space Mountain — a roller coaster — in the pitch dark. During the ride, something flipped inside of me and I decided I *hated* roller coasters. I tried to jump off the ride while it was moving. It took my dad every ounce of strength he had to hold me down until the ride ended. And he's a strong guy. Ever since, I've been terrified of roller coasters.

So, I was conflicted when Lorelei asked me to go with her to Kings Island. But when you are dating someone, you do things for them you normally wouldn't do for anyone else. I finally caved to her loving peer pressure under one circumstance — I was not riding any roller coasters. She agreed, and we went.

Of course, as soon as we got to the park, her tune changed. She wooed me on to some smaller rides at first. I'm pretty sure she was secretly trying to get me over my fear of roller coasters. After much pressure, I finally agreed to get on *The Beastie*. It was easily the scariest kids roller coaster at the park. Apparently, it used to be called *Scooby-Doo*, but in 1980 it was renamed in honor of their new world-renown wooden roller coaster — *The Beast*.1 I just couldn't understand how none of the eight-year-olds around me weren't scared to death.

As you already guessed, I survived *The Beastie*.

Interesting, isn't it? Our brains have a way of recalling traumatic memories when triggered. Sitting on that kids coaster, mine took me back to Space Mountain. And it was painful.

The rest of the afternoon Lorelei kept telling me how much she thought I would love riding *The Beast*. I told her just the name of the ride indicates the pure evil someone had when creating it. God wouldn't make something called *The Beast* and convince us it was good. But she kept pressuring me to ride it just *once* with her.

In that moment, I knew exactly why Samson gave in to Delilah. I'd like you to think I agreed to ride it with her because I care so much about making her happy. But that would be a lie.

The truth is, I was tired of being made fun of and felt compelled to prove my manhood. Isn't that what often gets us guys into trouble?

We stood in line for over an hour. With each step closer to the ride, I turned a different shade of green. I kept asking her if it had a big hill. She assured me it wasn't very big.

Now you can understand why I almost broke off the engagement. Her character was in question.

As we got close enough to see passengers being loaded on the ride, I could feel my heart rate climbing. I barely spoke a word to her the last ten minutes we were standing in line. I wanted to run away so badly, but I couldn't get out of the line without looking like a weenie.

Once we were strapped into the cart, there was no way to leave. With my pulse pushing 140, I took a deep breath — perhaps my last breath. Suddenly and violently, the cart jolted forward. I felt the chug, chug, chug of the cart going up the first hill, and immediately I knew — she had lied. I can't repeat some of the words I said in that moment. Let's just say they weren't very Christ-like. My spidey senses are telling me that some of you are judging me right now.

As the cart crested the hill, everything went silent. I couldn't breathe. My stomach was in my throat and my soul belonged to *The Beast*. I wonder if people who go to hell will feel this way for hours on their plummet into the lake of fire. That would cause weeping and gnashing of teeth for sure.

The wooden cart whipped us around, back and forth, back and forth for a few minutes before *finally* it slowed down.

I did it! *I had survived The Beast.*

I figured this would be one of those stories I would tell my grandkids when they crawled up on my lap. Now kids, let me tell you about the time your Poppy survived one of the most dangerous... You know how those stories go? Well, I thought that until the cart started to chug, chug, chug back up *another* big hill. Now I was furious.

"You never said there were *two* big hills!" I yelled.

My worst nightmare all over again. This really was the ride from hell.

Meanwhile, Lorelei was having the time of her life.

I survived riding *The Beast* and somehow our relationship survived, too. Over the years, I've been able to face my fear of roller coasters and have actually been able to enjoy some of them. I can proudly say I can ride all the roller coasters at the Disney World theme parks! That's a good thing since I find myself there a lot.

———————

In the world of faith, fear is a four-letter word.

Fear is often viewed as the antithesis of faith. We've created a dichotomy between fear and faith. Scores of Christians wear t-shirts or have coffee mugs that read, "Faith over Fear." Worship songs have been written declaring that fear is gone or has no place in the life of a believer or the presence of God. Social media posts constantly allude to fear as the enemy of faith. To be afraid is to lack faith and vice versa.

IN THE WORLD OF FAITH, *FEAR* IS A FOUR-LETTER WORD.

I'm not so sure we should put faith and fear in opposing camps. In fact, I would go so far as to say we might be creating a *false* dichotomy.

The opposite of faith is not fear.

The opposite of faith is *certainty*.

Let me remind you of how the Bible defines faith in Hebrews 11.

> Now faith is confidence in what we hope
> for and assurance about what we do not see.
> [Hebrews 11:1]

Let me rephrase that for us. Faith is having a confident trust *without* certainty. It's believing something will happen even if you can't prove it will. Faith is often a very allusive concept to grasp because it is not grounded on proof. It's like dark matter. We can't see it, but we know it's real.

One of my favorite examples of faith is found in Daniel 3. It's the story of three young Israelites who were taken captive to Babylon when Jerusalem was overthrown in the sixth century BC. Shadrach, Meshach, and Abednego had worked their way up to low-level management positions in the province of Babylon. The king of Babylon, Nebuchadnezzar, liked taking the youngest and brightest from nations he conquered, reindoctrinating them and putting them to work for him.

One day, King Nebuchadnezzar decided to have a ninety-foot golden statue erected in his honor. This was more than just a tribute to his name. It was an object of worship for all the subjects in his kingdom. The king issued an order. Whenever the band starts to play his theme song, everyone must fall to the ground and worship the image of gold. Anyone who refused to bow would be thrown into a blazing furnace. It would seem King Nebuchadnezzar saw himself more like a god than a king.

The problem for the three Israelites is that their religion forbids them from worshiping any other god but the God of Israel, Yahweh. To bow down and worship this image would be a direct violation of the Ten Commandments. They would refuse.

This infuriated the king. He gave them one last chance to bow down and asked the band to reprise the bridge and chorus. But the three men were wholly obstinate. How they responded in the face of certain death is perhaps the most faith-filled statement you will find in the Bible.

> Shadrach, Meshach and Abednego replied
> to him, "King Nebuchadnezzar, we do not
> need to defend ourselves before you in this
> matter. If we are thrown into the blazing
> furnace, the God we serve is *able* to

deliver us from it, and he *will*
deliver us from Your Majesty's hand. But
even if he does not, we want you to know,
Your Majesty, that we will not serve your
gods or worship the image of gold you have
set up."

[Daniel 3:16-18 emphasis mine]

That's bold.

That takes guts.

That's faith.

They brazenly announced to the king that the God they serve *is able* to deliver them. They believed an all-powerful God could step in and perform a miracle anytime He wanted. They trusted in God's *ability*.

Not only did they know God *could*, but they were also convinced He *would*. This was not a question of God's ability but His proclivity for the righteous. They trusted in God's *proclivity* for them.

But while they knew God *could* save them, and believed He *would*, they left room for God to choose *not* to rescue them.

213

They also believed it was possible that God's plan and purpose wasn't to rescue them. I love the bold statement they made.

Even if he does not... we will not serve or worship your gods. They trusted in God's *sovereignty*.

This is what faith looks like in practice. It's a bold confidence in God's ability, proclivity, and sovereignty *without* any certainty. Read that sentence again and let it sink in.

It's Noah building an ark even though it had never rained.

It's Abraham packing up his family and heading to an unknown destination.

It's Moses promising the Pharaoh an army of frogs are coming.

It's David charging at Goliath with a slingshot.

It's Peter stepping out on the water in the middle of a storm.

You can have faith and still be afraid.

It always surprises me to hear people say they think the Bible is boring. Sure, parts of it can be a bit repetitive or confusing. But when you begin to understand the overall theme, it becomes quite exciting.

What's more thrilling than the story of humanity discovering divinity? Ordinary people on a search for an extraordinary God? Unfortunately, we sometimes confuse the two and forget that these real heroes of faith were humans just like us.

James, the half-brother of Jesus reminds us of this truth.

> Elijah was a human being, even as we
> are. He prayed earnestly that it would not
> rain, and it did not rain on the land for three
> and a half years. Again he prayed, and the
> heavens gave rain, and the earth produced
> its crops.
>
> [James 5:17-18]

James is referring to a story we find in 1 Kings 17. The prophet Elijah delivered God's judgment to the king of Israel for leading the nation into idolatry. So, Elijah stood before the king and declared it would not rain again until the day he said it would. Then he dropped the mic and left the room.

We have to wait hundreds of years to find out exactly what Elijah did after leaving the king. James tells us Elijah prayed *earnestly* it would not rain. Now, why would you need to pray for it *not* to rain if God had already said it wouldn't?

Any guesses?

My guess is, he was afraid it just might.

Why else would he have to pray earnestly?

Surely Elijah wouldn't make that bold claim unless God sent him. But if it rained, Elijah would be considered a false prophet. The penalty for being a false prophet was death. Put yourself in a position where you have to trust God for supernatural results, and it will drive you to your knees. I am willing to bet if you or I were in Elijah's shoes we would be praying every waking moment.

"Dear God, please make it *not* rain today."

I would pray this prayer every hour while checking the sky for clouds.

For three and a half years, there was neither rain nor dew in the land. Elijah hid the entire time because King Ahab had scouting parties looking for him. Then one day, God told Elijah to confront King Ahab and tell him it was going to rain soon.

Before Elijah drops the news about rain, he confronts the very reason God held the rain back — idol worship. I'll give you the *CliffsNotes* version, but you should go read 1 Kings 18 on your own. It's epic!

Elijah challenges the prophets of Baal to a god-vs-God cage match in front of all the Israelites. Each side built an altar and put a bull on top of it for a sacrifice. Whichever deity responded by sending fire from heaven to consume the sacrifice won.

Elijah lets the prophets of Baal go first. Hours of chanting go by with no response. Either Baal was taking a nap, using the restroom, or is not a real god. Elijah's turn. He steps up and utters a simple prayer and fire falls from heaven and consumes the sacrifice. Elijah's hand is raised in victory! Elijah then calls for all 450 *false* prophets to be slaughtered. The moral of the story: you better make sure you heard God correctly before you speak on His behalf.

Now back to the rain.

With the fresh stench of prophet corpses filling the air, Elijah gives another prophetic word to Ahab. I love the way he says it too.

And Elijah said to Ahab, "Go, eat and
drink, for there is the sound of a heavy rain."
[1 Kings 18:41]

He basically tells the king to throw a party because rain is on the way. The only problem was the weather hadn't changed. In fact, there wasn't even a single cloud in the sky.

Once again, Elijah is forced to a posture of prayer. He gets on his knees with his face to the ground and prays with everything in him for God to send rain. Without looking up, Elijah sends his servant to look for any sign that God heard his prayer. It's possible Elijah was having such an incredible time of prayer he didn't want to get up. Or perhaps Elijah's faith couldn't stand the sight of a cloudless sky.

Every time Elijah sent his servant to look for a sign of rain, he was disappointed. I wonder if by the fifth or sixth time, Elijah started to panic. He'd just had 450 false prophets executed for... well, being false.

After a while, I wonder if his prayers sounded something like this.

"Um, hello God. Where's the rain? You told me to do this and now my butt is on the line. If you don't come through, I'm dead."

You see, Elijah operated in faith but also experienced the very real emotion of fear. We know this for sure because of what happens right after God sent a torrential downpour.

Word got to Queen Jezebel that Elijah had defeated her prophets and had all of them killed. She was livid and sent a threat to Elijah. She swore to hunt him down and kill him before sunset.

You would think a great man of faith like Elijah, who witnessed God shut the heavens for three and a half years and then made it rain fire with one prayer, wouldn't be scared of a measly threat. Instead, we discover this man of faith was scared to death.

Elijah was *afraid* and ran for his life.
[1 Kings 19:3a emphasis mine]

Again, this begs the question. Is it possible to be filled with faith and fear at the same time?

Do you think Shadrach, Meshach, and Abednego weren't afraid when they were being dragged toward the fiery furnace?

Do you think David wasn't even a little bit worried as he faced a giant warrior that ate people bigger than he was for breakfast?

And do you honestly think Peter wasn't terrified to step over the side of the boat in the middle of the storm?

Removing the humanity from these stories removes the essence of God's power working through them. All these men walked by faith *despite* their fear. Both can co-exist within us. We do not have to fall into the trap of a false dichotomy here. In fact, I would argue fear and faith have far more in common than not.

We've already addressed the fact that faith lives in the space of uncertainty. Faith is fully trusting in God even without knowing the outcome. I can trust God with my health and believe God for a healing without knowing if God will heal me now or in eternity.

Faith is stepping into the future with a hopeful *what if* spirit.

What if God does heal my mom?

What if my new business can provide jobs for many?

What if God opens the door I've been praying for?

What if God uses my scary faith to impact someone's eternity?

What if I, too, can walk on water?

Peter surely had a *what if* spirit of faith when he stepped over the side of the boat. He had no idea if he would sink or surf, but his faith postured him to believe the impossible.

But faith is not the only resident in the home of uncertainty. Worry, concern, doubt, and skepticism all live in the same dorm. And of course, we should also mention who lives at the end of the hall — fear.

Fear *also* lives in uncertainty. When we are fearful, our minds are also flooded with *what if* questions. These are the thoughts that keep us from taking any real risks.

What if she rejects my proposal?

What if I take this new job and hate it?

What if I pray for them and nothing happens?

What if I give away my emergency fund and something bad happens?

What if I can't really walk on water like Jesus?

Fear-filled questions like these can paralyze us.

Can you see it? Both faith and fear live in the same uncertain space. Perhaps fear and faith aren't mortal enemies like we've been told. We might have to accept that they are *bedfellows*. Though we are not always given insight into the emotional status of biblical heroes, it's hard to believe they didn't experience both fear and faith at the same time.

PERHAPS FEAR AND FAITH AREN'T MORTAL ENEMIES LIKE WE'VE BEEN TOLD.

Men like Gideon and Elijah had to wrestle through the internal battle of obedience to God and the fear of failure. This is the struggle you will face with every major faith decision. You will have to fight every urge in your body that's refusing to do what God is calling you to do.

Why? Because that's how God created your body to function.

You might think I'm a nerd for this, but I like neuroscience. Well, I kind of like all forms of science, but I'm especially fascinated by how our brains work. The more science continues to discover about how the human brain functions, the more I see the fingerprint of God on our lives.

Although I cannot scientifically prove where faith lives inside of us, I have a suspicion. Indulge me for a moment.

The human body is pre-wired for survival. Our most basic instinct is to stay alive at all costs. We have mechanisms in our brains that tell our bodies what to do when we experience fear.

Fear is a healthy and natural response to perceived forms of danger. This should dispel religious notions that fear comes from the devil. Fear is something God designed within us for our protection and it's quite brilliant. Fear is not just a spiritual issue, it's a biological one.

Fear has a home.

It lives in your *amygdala*.

The amygdala is made up of two almond-shaped clusters located within the limbic system. Our limbic system is responsible for behavioral and emotional responses, especially related to survival. Desires for eating, safety and reproduction are responses of the limbic system.2 We are designed with urges to eat in order to stay alive. Although far too often, we live to eat! Oh, and when you hear someone say their biological clock is ticking, it's their limbic system firing to ensure our species survives.

The amygdala is responsible for the *flight* or *fight* response of fear. If you run into a mountain lion while hiking in the woods, your amygdala will light up like a Christmas tree. Think of it like a massive warning sign going off for the rest of your brain.

A friend of mine, Dr. Wes Beavis, is a clinical psychologist who relies upon neuroscience research to help patients understand why they react in certain ways as a response to stress. One day he was describing to me what happens when fear activates our brains. I'll summarize the hour-long phone call.

When your amygdala fires it causes your body to release two important chemicals — *adrenaline* and *cortisol.*

Adrenaline is produced in your adrenal glands and is known as the stress hormone. When your body is stressed, adrenaline serves a vital function in your self-preservation. Adrenaline causes air passages to dilate so your muscles can get more oxygen. You'll need that if you are having to fight for your life or run from a threat. It also causes your blood vessels to contract to redirect blood to major muscles like your lungs or heart. This is why you might be in a fight and not feel pain from it until the adrenaline wears off. Your body is designed to survive, and adrenaline gives you the rush you need to handle those fearful or stressful situations.3

Cortisol is another hormone that is released to help you *focus* only on what is necessary under great duress. It shuts down certain functions to redirect all your focus to the threat in front of you. If you run into a mountain lion while hiking, the only thing you will think about is that lion and how to get to safety. Cortisol shuts down your growth processes, digestive system, and reproductive system under great stress. Basically, you won't waste brain power thinking about what to eat for dinner. Instead, you are simply trying not to *become* dinner.

All these functions are designed for self-preservation. Even if you are not standing face-to-face with a mountain lion, you can still have a similar response to a *perceived* threat. That means you don't have to be in any imminent danger to experience fear.

When we step out in faith for God, we know there is a chance we might fail. The perceived threat of embarrassment, loss, or even failure can cause us to freeze or run from what we feel called to do. In other words, your body will *naturally* resist operating in faith. It goes against our human predisposition for self-preservation. You will face an internal battle as your brain tries to keep you from stepping out of the boat onto the water.

But — and here's where everything changes — we can *choose* to move in faith even if fear is trying to stop us.

Peter shows us this is possible. His amygdala was surely firing the night Jesus called him onto the water. When the massive storm dropped on them in the pitch dark, the disciples thought they were going to drown. Adrenaline and cortisol were freely flowing through all of the disciples to help them survive the storm. I'm sure they got another dose of these chemicals as soon as they saw the ghost too.

Yet Peter still had the ability to put his leg over the side of the boat when Jesus said, "come." Peter decided to trust Jesus over what his amygdala was telling him. He had to throw an *override* switch in his brain to act in faith.

We, too, must learn to throw the override switch if we are going to fulfill our God-given purpose. God will call you to trust in him as you walk on the waters of uncertainty. Your amygdala is going to set your prefrontal cortex off with a ton of *what if* questions.

Back to the *prefrontal cortex* I mentioned in Chapter Four. This is the part of our brain that's responsible for executive functions, such as reason, logic, emotion control, and complex thought. You use your prefrontal cortex to think, plan, and make important decisions. Peter had to employ his prefrontal cortex when he decided to step out of the boat.

This part of your brain will lead you to process every faith-filled decision through the filter of logic. Every decision you make won't just be influenced by fear; it will also be influenced by logic. When the numbers don't add up or a decision seems to defy common sense, that is when you must decide what voice you will listen to. Will you listen to the voice of God or the voice in your head? By the way, I've often found God's voice will violate common sense.

> This is what Noah did when he built the ark even though it had never rained before. Surely people thought he had lost his marbles.

> This is what David did when he picked stones from a riverbed to face a giant warrior with a spear and sword. He was outgunned.

This is what Elijah did when he proclaimed it would rain after a three-and-a-half-year drought. The forecast was not on his side.

Right about now you might be thinking, "my anatomy is working against my faith." In a way, you are correct. Your spiritual enemy might not be your greatest hurdle to walking in faith; it might be your synapses. But keep in mind, the same faculties in your brain that tell you to *stay* in the boat are the same ones that can give you the courage to get *out* of the boat. The same tools that can work *against* you can be the very weapons of faith that work *for* you.

So, what was it that enabled all these heroes of faith to override their fear and choose to walk in courage? What gave Peter the ability to listen to the voice of Jesus over the synapses in his prefrontal cortex? The answer might seem a little too simplistic. It might even feel a bit cliché. But I think we need to hear it. Ready for it?

They all had an intimate relationship with God.

I know, you were probably expecting a more mysterious answer. But it's actually that simple.

Before they walked *in* faith, they walked *with* God.

David showed us his secret in this famous Psalm.

> Even though I *walk*
>> through the darkest valley,
>
> I will fear no evil,
>> for you are *with* me;
>>> [Psalm 23:4 emphasis mine]

There was plenty to fear in the darkest valleys of David's life. He spent years running for his life while being hunted by a jealous king. He faced war after war after he finally became the king of Israel. But David could walk in faith because he knew God was walking with him.

BEFORE THEY WALKED *IN* FAITH, THEY WALKED *WITH* GOD.

Your walk *with* God determines how much you walk *by* faith. Pause and read that sentence again. There is no magic formula, just the formation of a relationship with Jesus. The reason Peter could walk *on* water is because he walked *with* Jesus before that moment. It was his proximity to Jesus that enabled the power of his faith.

The way you build your faith muscles is by building your calf muscles.

One of my favorite stories from the book of Acts is found in chapter four. Two of Jesus' disciples, Peter and John, were arrested by the Jewish ruling council for preaching about Jesus' resurrection. They walked with a boldness and faith that was producing converts and miracles. After the council interrogated Peter and John, they came to this conclusion.

> When they saw the courage of Peter and
> John and realized that they were
> unschooled, ordinary men, they were
> astonished and they took note that these
> men had been *with* Jesus.
>
> [Acts 4:13 emphasis mine]

The ruling council was surprised to discover that these guys were uneducated and ordinary. It seems our English translators were being kind when they use the word *ordinary*. Luke, the original writer of the book of Acts used the Greek word *idiotes*.

Does it look like any English word you know?

You probably already guessed it.

It's what we derive our English word *idiot* from.

If you feel like you are just ordinary and don't have much to offer, the good news is you have all you need to do great exploits of faith. What's the key? The council saw it. I hope you can, too.

... they took note that these men had been *with* Jesus.

The disciples had been *with* Jesus so much they started to think and act like Him. Without even knowing it, faith was forming inside of them when they walked with Jesus.

The Apostle Paul goes even further to say faith initially comes to life inside us when we first hear the message of Jesus. The Good News of Jesus entering through our cochlea has the power to bring faith to life.

> So faith comes from hearing, that is, hearing
> the Good News about Christ.
> [Romans 10:17 NLT]

Any time you connect with God by reading the Bible, you are taking steps with Him.

Any time you pray and meditate on God's faithfulness, it's another step.

Any time you gather with a community to worship and engage with the preaching, you take more steps.

Any time you give generously to the work of God, you are catching your stride with Him.

Any time you share God's love with your co-worker, you are in step with God.

Any time you respond in obedience to something you feel God prompting you to do, it's walking with Him.

I know for many Christ followers, these disciplines can feel arduous and repetitive. Sometimes it feels like we are checking off the proverbial religious boxes when we do them. I rarely feel fireworks inside of me when I read my Bible or talk with God. But what we don't realize is each moment *with* Jesus is really building our faith. Whenever you set your mind in the direction of the all-powerful God, it enables you to believe anything is possible.

This isn't just spiritual alchemy; it's actual neurochemistry.

When I asked Dr. Beavis if there are any indicators of faith within our brains, he immediately told me about Dehydroepiandrosterone (DHEA). Try saying that three times fast!

DHEA is a hormone that causes neurogenesis, the process of creating neurons in the brain. DHEA plays a specific role during embryonic development but also continues throughout our lives. DHEA is a neurosteroid that can improve brain cognition and help with neuroplasticity, the ability for the brain to form and reform neural connections. This is why stroke victims can sometimes regain cognitive function over time. I love knowing God's creative power that forms us in our mother's womb is still creating and recreating within us in our post-natal stages.

DHEA is naturally produced in your adrenal glands but is also found in brain tissue. Your body uses it for many purposes. But in the brain, it helps reduce the negative effects of mood disorders, anxiety, and depression. It's such a powerful natural steroid it's believed DHEA can enhance athletic performance. Because of this, the World Anti-Doping Agency (WADA) has banned its use as a supplement by athletes in sports competitions.4 This, of course, is why I don't take it. Wouldn't want to jeopardize my future professional sports career, would I?

A study published by the journal *Nature* in 2013 shows that DHEA has a profound effect on connections between the amygdala and hippocampus, areas in the limbic system that play a significant role in our fear responses. This study indicated chemical levels in these areas that are connected to negative emotions were reduced when DHEA was released.

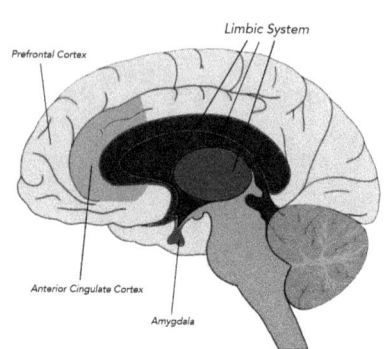

There is growing evidence that DHEA affects another area in the brain that connects our prefrontal cortex to our limbic system called the anterior cingulate cortex (ACC).5 Think of it as the neural highway between your thoughts (prefrontal cortex) and your emotions (limbic system). We might describe the anterior cingulate as the interpreter between these two areas. The anterior cingulate works to help us control and manage our emotions, make decisions, and handle social interactions.6 It's the bridge where our thoughts and our emotions come together to form our decisions.

I don't know if this excites you, but it does me. Okay, I may be a bit weird when it comes to science and faith, but I see an inseparable connection between our physiology and our spirituality! Let me try to pull it all together.

Our bodies are designed for survival. Our limbic system takes over to preserve us whenever we feel stress or fear. Chemicals are released to give our bodies super strength either to fight our threat or run from it. While this is helpful when confronted by a mountain lion in the wild, it's not helpful when God calls us to get out of the boat and follow him into the scary unknown. Fear is a paralyzer and will keep you from moving in the realm of faith. If fear has a home in our physiology, it lives in our amygdala.

However, our bodies are not designed to stay in this mode long. Adrenaline and cortisol are only intended to help you get to safety but can have harmful effects if continually released. When someone *lives* in fear, their limbic system is running on overdrive, and it is not healthy physically. It causes anxiety, depression, and other harmful emotions that have negative effects on our body and soul. Maybe the Apostle Paul was on to something when he said these words in 2 Timothy 1:7:

> For God has not given us a *spirit of fear*, but
> of power and of love and of a *sound mind*.
> [2 Timothy 1:7 NKJV emphasis mine]

God didn't design you to *live in fear*, and He has not given you a *spirit of fear*. Instead, Paul wrote that God has given us a *sound mind*. A quick study of the original language is a bit enlightening. The word Paul uses for a "sound mind" comes from the Greek word *sophron*. This word indicates someone who is of sound mind and senses. But it also means to *curb one's desires and impulses, to have self-control*.7

This is how you know the Holy Spirit inspired Paul to write this. Paul was a tentmaker. He would've had no way of knowing DHEA actually reduces the influence of our amygdala and restores us to our right or sound mind. Fear is loudest when cortisol levels are highest. But faith can be loudest when DHEA levels are highest.

Though I can't prove it, I believe Peter's *anterior cingulate* overrode his fear and gave his prefrontal cortex the power to step over the side of the boat. I'm sure that is exactly what you were thinking when you were spreading butter on your toast this morning. But stay with me. See, DHEA flowing freely to Peter's anterior cingulate gave him the courage to process his fear and yet still choose a faith response. Peter made a conscious decision to listen to the voice of Jesus over the voice of fear within him. Even if Peter wasn't able to clearly see it was Jesus with his eyes, he recognized His voice.

And I believe we can, too.

If fear lives in the amygdala, then faith lives in the anterior cingulate.

As you walk with Jesus, His voice becomes more powerful than the fear responses in your brain. Whether it's done physically through neuroplasticity or spiritually through our walk with Christ, our faith can grow. The key is what you set your mind *on*. Again, maybe Paul was on to something when he gave us a way to build our faith in Philippians 4.

> Be anxious for nothing, but in everything by
> prayer and supplication, with thanksgiving,
> let your requests be made known to
> God; and the peace of God, which surpasses
> all understanding, will guard your hearts and
> minds through Christ Jesus.
> Finally, brethren, whatever things are true,
> whatever things *are* noble, whatever
> things *are* just, whatever things *are* pure,

whatever things *are* lovely, whatever
things *are* of good report, if *there is* any
virtue and if *there is* anything praiseworthy—
meditate on these things.

[Philippians 4:6-8 NKJV]

Speaking to an anxious mind, Paul gives us a way to develop DHEA in order to reduce our fear response. He invites us to bring every situation to God in prayer. When we learn to walk with God in every situation, even the darkest valleys, we experience the supernatural peace of God. But then Paul gives us an exercise that neuroscientists and therapists have found instrumental in mental health. He tells us to *meditate* on the right things. To focus our thoughts on that which is true, noble, and of good report. And in Colossians 3, Paul instructs us to "set our mind on things above this world" (Colossians 3:2).

In the world of therapy, this practice is called *mindfulness*. In the world of science, it's believed that positive or faith-filled thoughts can release DHEA into our system. John Hopkins has released research that shows a link between health and positivity.8 A twenty year study of middle-aged adults done at Yale University showed those with a positive view of aging lived more than seven and a half years longer than those with a negative view.9 Though scientists aren't exactly sure how setting your mind on positive things affects our physical health, they agree it absolutely does.

Of course, for thousands of years, we've known that when you set your focus and thoughts on the power and presence of God, it does something in us. Physiologically, it may release DHEA into our bodies. Spiritually, it releases faith into our spirit.

———————————

I believe we can operate in faith while learning to manage our fear. I have continually had to confront my fears while choosing to *move* in faith. This is the full expression of *Scary Faith*. I believe we will experience fear when we choose to walk in faith. I reject the idea that to have faith is to not be afraid. I believe they both take up residence in us.

One time I was being vulnerable around one of our church members regarding the decision to build our new multimillion-dollar facility. This person responded by reminding me of the all the sermons I've preached on faith. As if I was supposed to not be afraid if I had real faith.

This tends to be the traditional Christian mindset when it comes to fear and faith. I would argue, the real question isn't which one we have. It's which one will we listen to. I can move in faith even if I'm scared to death of what might happen.

Peter got out of the boat scared. The important thing is that he took the step, not how scared he was while taking it. Don't let anyone tell you that isn't faith. Your faith is real when you make real decisions that have real consequences.

The key is learning to walk with Jesus and build your faith *daily*. There is no shortcut to building faith. And in your walk with Christ, He will call you to new steps of faith. Every small step of faith we take prepares us to take a bigger one.

My question for you is this:

Have you responded in obedience to the small step God has put in front of you?

God might be asking you to give a full tithe (ten percent) to your church or get out of a dating relationship that doesn't honor him or boldly share your faith with an unsaved neighbor. While it might not seem like a big thing, what you can't see is how God wants to build your faith for what's next. Each step will get bigger until one day you find yourself standing in your God-given purpose.

May I suggest some exercises to increase your DHEA levels?

- Create a rhythm of reading God's Word daily. Even if you don't feel fireworks, make it a priority.
- Write down your God-inspired dreams and begin to pray for them out loud.
- Take just five minutes each day to set your mind on God's infinite ability to provide everything you need for the dream He has given you. Wrap this in an expression of gratitude and praise.
- Attend a local church weekly so you can encounter the presence of God and have a community to help you build your faith.
- Memorize Ephesians 3:20 and declare it every day in prayer.

Now to Him who is able to do exceedingly
abundantly above all that we ask or
think, according to the power that works in us,
[Ephesians 3:20 NKJV]

11

EMBRACE THE MYSTERY

"The most beautiful experience we can have is the mysterious. It is the source of all true art and all true science. Whoever does not know it, who can no longer pause to wonder or stand rapt in awe, is as good as dead."

~ *Albert Einstein*

I LIVED IN GERMANY for three years when I was in high school. Those were some of the best years of my life and the first time I got to see the world outside of America. I had been to Mexico once prior to this, but somehow that didn't quite feel as international. At the time, I didn't fully appreciate what a privilege it was to live and travel through Europe. What do you expect? I was a teenager and quite happy sitting in the house playing video games.

My parents were intentional about forcing us to take trips throughout Europe during our time over there. Horrible parents, huh? We traveled to Italy, Spain, France, Belgium, the Czech Republic, Luxemburg, Austria, Switzerland, and the Netherlands. I look back now, forever grateful they made us see the world.

Although I spent my early years living on both the East and West Coast, I spent most of my life in Ohio. The Buckeye State has its own charm and beauty. But it's not Germany-beautiful. To this day, Germany is still my favorite country in Europe.

If Germany is still my favorite place in Europe, the Zugspitze is still my favorite place in Germany. The Zugspitze is part of the Alps and the tallest peak in Germany at just under 10,000-feet above sea-level. It's my favorite place because of the view. Not from the bottom, but from the top.

Our family traveled there on a typical German summer day, partly cloudy and not too hot. My parents bought tickets for us to ride in a cable car to the summit. It's kind of like being in an enclosed ski lift with a dozen people while you go up the face of a mountain. Sound thrilling? Hard to believe that doesn't bother me but riding on a roller coaster does! But trust me, if you are ever in Germany, you have to do this. It's worth every penny of your parents' money.

When I stepped out of the cable car, it was as if I had just walked through a magical coat closet into another world. I don't really have any words to describe the view. It literally took my breath away. The air was cold and thin and cut right through me. I discovered that the sky is a different shade of blue when the clouds are dancing beneath your feet. Gray rock sheers draped in white snowy blankets filled my senses in all directions. Below were green rolling hills and a turquoise lake that looked more like a backyard pond from that height. At the base of the mountain were ant-like figures scurrying in all directions. It took me a few moments to realize those ants... were people.

At the top of the Zugspitze, I felt small. Really small. And God felt big. Really big. Take a drive through the Alps and you will be impressed. Stand on top of them and you will feel something entirely different.

The only word I can think to describe this moment is *majestic*. In one sense, I've never felt closer to God and yet in another He never felt further away. When you grow up around faith, God becomes part of your world rather than you part of His. We can be tempted to treat God like an imaginary friend, as if He is Casper the ghost rather than God the Creator. That day God became much bigger to me. My predefined Christian box was opened, and I had to let Him out.

> The heavens declare the glory of God;
>> the skies proclaim the work of his
> hands.
> Day after day they pour forth speech;
>> night after night they reveal knowledge.
> They have no speech, they use no words;
>> no sound is heard from them.
> Yet their voice goes out into all the earth,
>> their words to the ends of the world.
>> [Psalm 19:1-4]

There is far more mystery than understanding when it comes to faith. I'm guessing hundreds, if not thousands, of books have been written attempting to explain faith. Most of them are filled with insightful theological expositions far better than I can give. I'm not a theologian or theorist; I'm a practitioner. I write these things from my understanding of Scripture, my experience as a pastor, and my personal journey of faith.

I'm not sure any of us can *fully* understand faith. In fact, I'm not even sure we are supposed to. Don't let any preacher make you think they've got it all figured out. The shroud of mystery that surrounds faith will never be removed on this side of eternity. My guess is God wants it that way. Perhaps deep down inside, we do too.

Do you love watching movies?

My favorite type of movie is one with some action, adventure, a lot of suspense, and a surprise ending. I hate when movies are too predictable. I want to be surprised. My wife, on the other hand, has to know what a movie is about *before* she watches it. She won't watch it before reading the entire premise first. But not me. I like the mystery of discovering the plot within the story.

We may not all agree on our favorite movies, but I think we can all agree there is nothing worse than someone spoiling the end of one. I can't stand watching a movie with *that* guy. You know, the kind of person who drops hints as to whether the main character dies, overcomes the struggle, or falls in love. I don't want to know what is going to happen *before* it happens. I want to find out at the end. That's part of the experience.

Maybe in a way, we all crave that same experience out of life, not just with movies. Would you really want to know *how* or *when* your life is going to end? I guess if you really want to know you can visit *deathclock.com* and find out. It's a website that calculates the day you are going to die. Here's a little secret... it doesn't really know. I'm not so sure I would make all your life's plans based on those results.

If we had an actual death clock counting us down to the moment our heart stopped, I'm not sure we would ever truly live. Yes, we might do all the things on our bucket list, but my guess is we wouldn't do the things on *God's* bucket list. We would focus more on what we could *get* out of this life rather than what we could *do* with it. In the end, the only way to truly live is to invest in your eternal future and build something here on earth that will never be taken away.

WE DESIRE MYSTERY MORE THAN WE CARE TO ADMIT.

I believe we desire mystery more than we care to admit. Yes, I know most of us don't like facing uncertainty, especially when talking about our future. We'd all love to know when we will get promoted, not wonder if we ever will. Who wouldn't want to know how their investments will perform over the next twenty years on the stock market? If I had a DeLorean, I too would probably head back to the future to see what my life turns out to be. But that's in the movies. This is real life. We don't know. And we never will. While it makes life harder, it also makes life sweeter.

Not knowing when or how he will propose makes the moment even more special. Not knowing in advance your spouse was throwing you a huge surprise party for your birthday makes you feel even more cherished. Not knowing exactly when your child will take her first step is part of the thrill of parenthood. It's the unexpected moments of laughter and surprise that fill our hearts with joy. If the mystery of this life was removed, we would find it dull and uninspiring. Even if you hate surprises, I promise you would hate life without them.

This is what it means to be human in a world we didn't create.

Universities and laboratories are full of brilliant minds trying to unpack the mysteries of life. And yet after centuries of technological advancements in astronomy, physics, and mathematics, we still don't have a clue how the universe got its start or what the meaning of it all is to begin with.

But if we are not careful, we might spend so much energy trying to decode the mystery of our world that we miss the beauty of it. We can squander our time peering through a telescope or microscope and yet never fully appreciate what we are observing. It would be like standing at the edge of the Grand Canyon so perplexed over its origin that you miss the gorgeous sunset over the desert backdrop in front of you.

Don't try to figure everything out.

Don't miss the sunset.

Just enjoy it.

In many ways I wish I could become a kid again. The less you know, the more you enjoy life. To a kid, the world is full of endless possibilities. When I was little, I used to run around my grandparents' house in Virginia pretending I was a superhero. I could fly, fight off twenty bad guys with my karate skills, and destroy things with my laser vision. I wasn't bound by gravity or any of the universal laws that make us human. I was a super-human, able to do good and save the world.

Back in the 1960s, a scientific study actually gave us some fascinating hints about the wonder and creativity we begin to lose as our childhood fades. George Land, PhD, is probably best known for the formation of the transformation theory, a theory of natural processes that integrates principles of creativity, growth, and change. In 1965, he founded a research and consulting institute to study the enhancement of creative performance.1 Basically, he was an expert in studying creativity.

NASA contacted Dr. Land and his associate, Beth Jarman, and asked them to develop a highly specialized test to measure the creative ability of their rocket scientists and engineers. NASA needed a way of knowing which employees would prove to be the best in terms of creativity. The test was so predictive it led them to ask a deeper question. Where does the potential of creativity come from? Are some born more creative than others or is it something that is developed with the right environment? In other words, is creativity developed from nature or nurture?

Dr. Land and Jarman administered this same test to 1600 children from ages four to five, and the results were shocking. Ninety-eight percent of the children scored at the genius level. They determined that we are all geniuses at some point in our lives. Even if you don't feel like it now, at one point you probably were one.

They gave the test again to those same 1600 children five years later. This time only 30% of the children fell into the genius category when it came to creativity. Once more, they administered the same test to these children at age fifteen and found that only 12% of them still registered at the genius level. When they were given this test as adults, only 2% scored in the genius category.2 As adults, we've exchanged a world of endless possibilities for a world of limited plausibility.

There's clearly a connection between learning more and losing more of our creativity and imagination. How sad! Maybe this is why we tend to lose our wonder as we grow up. This might explain why kids dream of becoming doctors, firefighters, and other roles that serve the public and save lives but often settle for jobs that pay the bills and create a safe lifestyle. We have somehow created an environment where our kids exchange what they want to *be* for what they want to *have*.

This is a bad exchange.

When the mystery of life is removed, so is our desire to change the world. The more we know, the less we dream. The more we understand about the natural world, the less we believe in the supernatural world.

I believe God is looking for people who still dream of unknown possibility and have the faith to believe that *with God* all things are possible. He's looking for those who embrace the mystery of faith and aren't afraid to risk everything they have to attain something even greater.

I believe at our core we still long for a world filled with mystery. It's the uncertainty of life that is a double-edged sword. It's wondering if we may get promoted that keeps us working harder. It's hoping this relationship may lead to a wedding that gives us butterflies inside. It's the excitement of meeting your soon-to-be born baby that enables you to endure the pregnancy. That's one side of the sword.

The other side of uncertainty is what so often paralyzes us and keeps us from our destiny. We won't break off a dysfunctional relationship because we are afraid of being alone. We won't risk starting something new because we are afraid it might fail. We stay stuck in a dead-end job because it's familiar and to do something else is frightening.

We love mystery but we crave certainty. We tend to cave to our basic instinct for self-preservation. Yet I believe certainty is a chain around our ankles. We allow the fetters of our past to keep us from taking that scary, faith-filled step over the edge of the boat. We often think staying in the boat is safer than venturing out onto the water. Yet, we don't realize that the boat is slowly sinking our soul. The routine and meaningless life we abhor is sucking the awe and wonder from our spirit.

We crave certainty over creativity. We settle for what's practical and give up what's possible. We don't realize it, but our desire for safety has created a small hole in our plastic aquarium. The goldfish is unaware that the very substance of his breath is leaking out of the bottom. His life is draining out slowly only to find that

WE CRAVE CERTAINTY OVER CREATIVITY.

one day he can't move, let alone breathe. When life resorts to the irreducible minimum, that is when our faith goes on a ventilator.

Faith is like a muscle; it's either growing or shrinking. Muscles grow when worked but atrophy when stagnant.

Several years ago, my father was in a motorcycle accident that broke his kneecap and tore ligaments in his leg. He had surgery to repair it and was forced to keep his leg in a fixed position for several weeks while it healed. When he started with physical therapy, he discovered that one of his legs was thinner than the other. While in the cast, his muscles atrophied, and he lost an immense amount of strength.

Is your faith in a cast?

When was the last time you exercised your faith?

When was the last time you did something so scary that if God didn't show up you were in trouble?

When was the last time your heart raced and palms sweat because you had no idea if you would fail?

What would you do today if you knew God was with you?

What bold move would you make if you knew you couldn't fail?

Could you fail? Sure. Peter knew that. But he also walked on the water. Yes, Peter started to sink, but Jesus wouldn't let him drown. But do you know what might be worse than failing? Regret for not trying.

My first year in full-time ministry, I told God I would go big or go home but I wouldn't play it safe. I was willing to take bold steps of faith and risk failure, but I was not willing to settle for a safe, cushy ministry job. Later that same year, I became so frustrated our church wasn't growing, I gave God an ultimatum.

"If something doesn't change within a year, I quit," I clamored.

He didn't respond.

Yes, I know I should never give the Creator of the Universe an ultimatum. But I was frustrated and a bit depressed. Thankfully, God was merciful to me, and something drastic changed when our church moved to Lithopolis *exactly* one year later. (God has a funny sense of humor.) I have always been more willing to bet the farm in hopes God does a miracle than to retire safely on the farm of mediocrity.

I know it's scary. Faith by its very nature *is* scary. I might be going too far with this next statement, but I believe it's true.

If it isn't scary, it probably isn't faith.

Or let me say it a little bolder. If it doesn't scare you, it probably doesn't impress God. If what you are attempting can be resolved using your own resources, it doesn't require faith or God. But if God is calling you to do something that seems impossible

IF IT ISN'T SCARY, IT PROBABLY ISN'T *FAITH*.

or beyond your capability, you, my friend, are standing at the edge of faith.

How can we embrace the mystery of faith with no guarantee we will survive?

The answer is found in the very words God put on repeat for Joshua.

> "Have I not commanded you? Be strong and courageous. Do not be afraid; do not be discouraged, for the Lord your God *will be with you* wherever you go."
>
> [Joshua 1:9 emphasis mine]

The reason Joshua could walk in confidence and courage is because of this one promise. And I believe this promise wasn't just for Joshua but all who answer God's call. Jesus reassured His disciples of this same promise right before He was arrested and crucified. Jesus knew His time on earth was up and gave His disciples the promise of His presence through the Holy Spirit.

> I will not leave you as orphans; I will come to you.
>
> [John 14:18]

We do not have any guarantee of success. But we have the promise of God's presence. Wherever you walk and whatever you do, God is with you. He will be near you so that if you fall, He will be there to catch you.

Can I declare that same promise over your life right now?

Place your name in the blank below and receive this promise today.

_____ , the Lord your God will be with you wherever you go!

That's a promise.

Take it to the bank.

Live like it's true.

12

LIVE A BETTER STORY

"Make your life a story worth telling."
~ Adam Braun

P ETER'S LIFE WAS ANYTHING but boring. Prior to meeting Jesus, he started a fishing business with his two friends, James, and John. The first moment he encountered Jesus, Peter hauled in such a huge catch it probably would have given him stability for a few months. Then he just walked away from it all to follow a Rabbi for three years.

He watched Jesus miraculously heal the sick, lame, blind, deaf, and diseased. He witnessed Jesus raise at least three people from the dead during those three years. And Peter quickly became part of Jesus' succession plan.

I imagine Peter never saw his life heading in a new direction. All he knew was fishing. He probably figured he would spend the rest of his days dredging the Sea of Galilee for tuna. Until the day he met Jesus. That day not only changed his life, it changed his story. It's almost unbelievable to think we are talking about an uneducated fisherman who lived 2,000 years ago. But what you should know is that his story almost fell off the pages of history.

Peter was that guy in the group who always spoke up first and said what was on his mind. He's the one you sometimes wish would think before he spoke. But with Peter, you also knew where you stood and wanted him to stand with you. When Jesus told his disciples He would soon be arrested and put to death, Peter stood up and said something to the effect of, "Not on my watch." He was brash, aggressive, and always ready to scuffle.

When Jesus was arrested, Peter reached for a sword and tried to cut the head off one of the assailants. He missed but managed to lop off an ear. Jesus stopped Peter and healed the guy's ear.

Such a Jesus move.

After Jesus was arrested, Peter had his lowest moment. While the religious leaders were interrogating Jesus, Peter hung out in the courtyard to keep an eye on the proceedings. Some of the patrons recognized him as one of Jesus' followers. Every time someone asked if he knew Jesus, he denied it. By the third time, others were convinced when he began to swear and cuss like the sailor he once was.

But when Peter heard the rooster crow, he immediately remembered what Jesus had predicted earlier that evening. Jesus told Peter he would deny Him three times before the rooster crowed. Peter failed the loyalty test. When the pressure mounted, he caved. The moment the rooster crow echoed in his ears, Peter felt unbearable shame and guilt. He had just denied even knowing Jesus, the One who changed his name, his life, and his future. Peter ran away and wept.

My guess is you've probably heard the Easter portion of Jesus' story. If you are only familiar with eight-pound baby Jesus from the Christmas narrative, the Easter part of His story is even better. They crucified Jesus and laid His lifeless body in a tomb. But on the third day, God raised Jesus back to life. It's the most significant historical moment ever and the foundation for

Christianity. The reason we believe God can and still does miracles is because of what happened to Jesus.

I can't imagine what it must have been like to find out the Rabbi you'd been following for the last three years really was the Son of God. Seeing Jesus resurrected must have been the most exhilarating thing ever. And yet you couldn't tell it from their reaction because I'm pretty sure they were in shock. You'd think they would be used to seeing Jesus as a ghost.

Jesus appeared to the disciples two times over the next week to encourage them and tell them to head back to Galilee. Those were also the same instructions Jesus gave them before He was arrested. Sometimes they were a little slow. The disciples did eventually travel back to Galilee, but something was wrong with Peter. He wasn't his usual self. Everyone saw it. He wasn't joking around anymore, and now he always walked with his head down.

Then one day he speaks up, revealing what is really in his soul.

> Simon Peter said, "I'm going fishing."
> [John 21:3]

I know what you are thinking. I thought Peter left that fishing business behind him. He did. But now he is going back to it. Although Jesus invited Peter into a greater destiny, he resorted back to what he knew. Why, Peter? John's account doesn't say, but I have a good guess.

Shame.

Peter messed up. He denied even knowing Jesus. That's not just an accounting error or leadership mistake. He betrayed God. In Jesus' darkest hour, Peter turned his back on Him. Is there anything worse?

Peter couldn't stomach what he had done. He couldn't even look Jesus in the eye let alone imagine ever being used by God. Now, all Peter could do was try to pick up the pieces of his *old* life. After Jesus' resurrection, the only thing Peter wanted to resurrect was his fishing business.

I would imagine some of you reading this can relate. In fact, I'm sure all of us can. We have all done things we are convinced has disqualified us from being used by God.

You got a divorce.

You have a record.

You filed bankruptcy.

You flunked out of school.

You got fired.

You have an addiction.

Like Peter, we all have things in our lives that bring us guilt and perhaps even shame. It might not be something from your past. It could be something you are living with right now.

So, I need you to hear this next statement clearly.

Stop any distractions and just read it.

Then marinate on it.

There is *nothing* you have done that separates you from God's love or His purpose for your life.

Receive it.

The story of God's love is the story of grace. It's you and me getting what we don't deserve. Let these words penned by the very guy who hunted down and imprisoned Jesus' followers rest in your soul.

> For it is by *grace* you have been
> saved, through *faith* — and this is not from
> yourselves, it is the gift of God — not by
> works, so that no one can boast.

[Ephesians 2:8-9 emphasis mine]

The reason Paul could write these words is because he was a trophy of God's grace.

So am I.

And so are you.

It's not because of you that God saves you; it's because of Jesus. Let me say this with all the humility I have. You will *never* be good enough to make up for all you've done. If you are trying to do that, stop. It's a waste. Instead, recognize what God is offering you right now — His amazing grace. It's a gift, wrapped in the death of Jesus. And there's really only three things you can do with a gift...

Open it.

Receive it.

Enjoy it.

But we can't stop there. We have to read the very next verse. This gift isn't just to cleanse you of your sin. It's also an invitation to live a better story.

For we are God's handiwork, created in
Christ Jesus to *do* good works, which God
prepared in advance for us to do.

[Ephesians 2:10 emphasis mine]

Jesus doesn't just save you *from* something; He saves you *for* something. Even if you don't feel this way, you need to hear this. You are still God's masterpiece. God formed you with a purpose. He wrote you into His story so that you could live a better story. God desires to take the broken pieces of your life and use them for His good works.

———————

Peter went fishing and many of the other disciples followed him. Peter was a leader even if he was leading people in the wrong direction. They tried to catch fish all night but caught nothing. That's when a silhouette from the shore yelled out to them, "throw your net on the right side of the boat and you will find some" (John 21:16).

They didn't find some; they found 153 of them to be exact. Their nets were so full they couldn't even haul them back onto the boat. A good problem to have. The fact that John counted how many fish they caught is telling. Perhaps this time, John wasn't going to walk away from the catch without first making a little dinero.

But for Peter, it was déjà vu all over again. He had a flashback to the last time he went fishing all night and caught nothing. Jesus told him to try it one more time. A miracle happened.

Peter couldn't stand it. He had to confront the elephant in the room and the man on the shore. He threw his outer cloak on and jumped into the water to swim for land. Unfortunately, Peter never mastered water walking and had to resort to freestyle.

As Peter stood on the beach soaking wet, the other disciples pulled up behind him in their rented boats. Jesus invited them to breakfast and told them to bring some of the fish they caught. Peter and John grabbed a few fish that were still flopping around and slowly walked up to Jesus' campfire. It probably seemed strange that Jesus asked them to bring some of their fish because He already had some trout on a skewer. My guess is Jesus wanted them to bring the fish they caught for a sermon illustration.

> When they had finished eating, Jesus said to
> Simon Peter, "Simon son of John, do you
> love me more than these?"
>
> [John 21:15a]

Ah yes, the sermon illustration. Jesus must have pointed to the fish they slid along the sand. But notice how Jesus addresses Peter in this situation. He called him "Simon" again. When Peter resumed fishing, he also assumed his old identity. Shame drug him back into his old life. Simon Peter was stuck between his past and his future. Jesus was giving him a choice. Will he go back to being Simon the fishermen, or move forward as Peter the fisher of men?

Peter's response proved how he felt about Jesus. He was just living in shame.

> "Yes, Lord," he said, "you know that I love
> you."
>
> [John 21:15b]

Jesus didn't need to hear Peter say the words. Peter needed to hear Peter say those words.

Jesus said, "Feed my lambs."

[John 21:15c]

Jesus was reminding Peter that he wasn't created to fish. He was called to shepherd. In fact, Jesus ends up asking Peter this same question three times in a row to erase the three times Peter denied Jesus.

In this exchange of grace, Jesus reinstates Peter.

This moment cannot be overstated. This didn't happen because Peter stopped believing in Jesus. This happened so Peter would know that Jesus never stopped believing in him. If there was any doubt before, Jesus made sure it was completely erased.

Jesus wasn't done with Peter.

And if I could say this to you — He's not done with you either!

———

In the Prologue, I mentioned that I'm living in the middle of my story of faith right now. As I write this, I do not know what will happen with our church in the months to come. We opened our new facility in the middle of a pandemic with an expectation of seeing significant growth in the first year. We haven't been able to see that growth yet.

I wish I could tell you we have millions of dollars in the bank to sustain us through this challenging season. But we don't. What reserves we do have are dwindling every month. We have some property for sale that could help, but in this economic climate very few are taking the risk on development.

Yet somehow, I still believe God will provide for us. I don't know how or where it will come from, but I believe it is on the way. I'm living in the land of uncertainty, and it's filled with faith and fear. I feel the weight of it every day like an anchor fastened to my soul. If I put my focus on these conditions, I will surely start to sink. This is the lesson Peter learned when he was out on the water.

> But when he saw the wind, he was afraid
> and, beginning to sink, cried out, "Lord,
> save me!" Immediately Jesus reached out his
> hand and caught him. "You of little
> faith," he said, "why did you doubt?" And
> when they climbed into the boat, the wind
> died down.

[Matthew 14:30-32]

The moment Peter took his eyes off Jesus and put it on the conditions of the storm, he began to sink. I cannot spend my days thinking about how big the gap is between what we need and what we have. That is putting my focus on the wind and the waves. That will drown my faith.

I'm discovering faith isn't just what prompts you to step out of the boat. It's also what sustains you with every step after that. I am learning to walk by faith and not by sight. I wish I could tell you it gets easier. I would love to tell you that as your faith grows, fear shrinks. But that hasn't been my experience. Instead, it seems more like when your faith grows, God increases the size of your next step.

How rude, right?

Maybe if we understood what pleases God, our paradigm of faith would change completely. The writer of Hebrews frames it this way:

> And it is impossible to please God *without* faith. Anyone who wants to come to him

must believe that God exists and that he
rewards those who sincerely seek him.

[Hebrews 11:6 NLT emphasis mine]

Faith isn't just for religious leaders or the super-spiritual.
Faith is necessary for any of us to please God. Imagine that you
pray every day, live an honest life, are involved in a local church,
and serve regularly. Still, you may never please God. God is not
impressed with religious piety. He's pleased with bold faith. God
places that high of a value on faith.

FAITH ISN'T JUST FOR *RELIGIOUS LEADERS* OR THE *SUPER-SPIRITUAL*.

Peter almost walked himself right out of his story. It's
only days later that Peter preaches the first sermon at the launch of the Church and 3,000 people are
saved. Peter would spend the rest of his days building the church,
preaching the Gospel to thousands, healing the sick, and raising
the dead. The reason we are still talking about Peter today is
because he chose sheep over fish.

He chose to walk in faith rather than work with fish.

———————

Though the Bible is complete, God's story is still being written. You and I have a part to play in the story God is writing. The question is, will you allow God to write you into His story (history)?

I don't know about you, but I want my life to be part of a bigger story. I want the purpose of my life to matter beyond my few years here on earth. I have a feeling you do, too.

You don't have to be called to full-time ministry to feel this way. We are all called and commissioned to be witnesses for Jesus. You can make an impact wherever God takes you. His purpose for your life is just as exciting as the one He has for me.

I once heard someone ask this question and I have never forgotten it.

Is your life a story worth telling 100 years from now?

That's a humbling question. In a way, I don't want to think I'm so special that people should still be talking about me a century later. But I hope what I *did* with my life creates a story worth telling 100 years from now.

Speaking of which, did you hear the story of the guy who made a great salary, lived in a large house in a great neighborhood, and drove a Mercedes? No? Neither did I. Can I be honest with you? That's not even a compelling story. A story that's not worth telling is a story that's not worth living.

When our goal in life is to live comfortably, we stop living. But when our only goal is to chase our God-given purpose, that is when we experience life to the fullest. Life with Jesus should be the greatest adventure you can imagine. Somehow in America we've adopted a version of Christianity that isn't compelling or convincing to the world around us. We've let faith become no more than just another noun. We've settled for comfort and convenience rather than audacious, courageous faith that leads us to experience the impossible.

A STORY THAT'S NOT WORTH *TELLING* IS A STORY THAT'S NOT WORTH *LIVING*.

Don't settle for that life.

Live a better story.

If you don't believe me, read the book of Acts in the New Testament. God used men and women to perform miracles, cast out demons, baptize thousands, and start churches all over the known world. Literally, they changed the world forever.

I'm convinced God wants to use me to change my world. I'm equally convinced God wants to use *you* to change *your* world. He wants to do miracles for you and through you. But you have to put yourself in the position of needing those miracles. And the only way you can do that is by listening to the voice of God and stepping out onto the water.

Today, God is inviting you to step onto the uncertain waters of your destiny. You will face storms and it will be scary. But it will also be the greatest adventure of your life. One day, you will look back on your life wondering how you got to where you are. Only then will you see that your journey took you to places you never dreamed possible.

Perhaps, allow the words of this passage to sink deeply into your soul as you ponder what could be around the horizon.

This resurrection life you received from God
is not a timid, grave-tending life. It's

adventurously expectant, greeting God with
a childlike "What's next, Papa?"

[Romans 8:15 MSG]

So, can I ask you some direct questions?

Does what you are doing right now matter?

If you died tomorrow, would you be satisfied with the life
you've lived?

Are you making this world, or your world, a better place?

If you don't know the answer to these questions, then
maybe it's time you and God had a conversation. Perhaps it's time
to ask your Heavenly Father what's next. Because I truly believe
that God has *more* in store for you and me. And He's waiting for
us to move in faith

My prayer is that while reading this book, you felt the
Spirit of God stirring something fresh within your spirit. Perhaps
the dream you let go of in your twenties or thirties is being
reignited right now! Maybe the burden you've felt for the last
couple years is surfacing again. The question is, will you respond
or shrink back down into the boat?

I know, it's scary.

But this is the life we've been called to.

This is what it means to live a better story.

So, reach for the edge of the boat, lift your legs over the side, place your soles on the surface of the deep, and... then... take a step.

EPILOGUE

S ITTING ON A RUST-COLORED, padded wicker chair — my current writing haven — with a Diet Citrus Green Tea within reach and my MacBook pressing firmly into my thighs with every keystroke, I typed out the final sentence of *Scary Faith*. My conscious stream of thoughts came to a sudden halt, and I finally noticed the erratic gawking of a small brown swallow perched in her nest above me.

It was a warm Thursday afternoon. (June 17, 2021, to be exact.) I took a deep breath and closed my eyes to take in the moment, opened them, and hit the Save button. Finished. I shut the laptop and a sense of relief washed over my soul. I knew I was supposed to share my journey of faith, even if I was still in the *middle* of it and had no idea how it would end. I still don't.

I don't know if you believe God still does miracles, but I do. No, I haven't seen Him part rivers or multiply dough (preferably in our bank account). But I have experienced moments that seem too good to call coincidence. Moments that remind me that God won't let us drown.

In the seven months that have passed since I finished this manuscript, I have witnessed miracles of God's provision. Reminiscent of the way God provided for the nation of Israel in the wilderness, our church has seen God provide *just enough* for the journey. His provision seems to show up in the 11th hour. But it *always* shows up.

The day after I finished writing this book, I received an email from our realtor, Matt. He forwarded me a Letter of Interest from a developer for the property we had listed for sale. Selling those five acres would replenish our cash flow significantly, allowing us time to grow both numerically and financially. This property had been on the market for over a year with zero interest. Now, all of a sudden, someone was seriously interested.

I tried not to let myself get too hopeful. This piece of land was almost in contract five years earlier. When that deal fell, it was a dagger through my heart. Yet, here I was, one day after finishing the book I felt God prompted me to write, and we had movement again. Perhaps God was up to something.

Three days after completing *Scary Faith*, a new friend from Atlanta, Joel, came to preach at our church. I think we connected over our common bond of being church planters. He had just planted COR Church earlier that year. I've joked with him as to who was crazier — me, for launching a brand-new building in the middle of a pandemic, or him, for launching a brand-new church in it. All I know is both of us are walking on the water right now.

Joel needed a new space for his church to meet. The place they were currently renting only held about fifty adults and had no air conditioning. Did I mention they were based in Atlanta? Muy caliente!

Joel had an opportunity to rent a school for their church starting in August. The only problem was he needed to raise at least $30,000 to make the transition. For a small startup-church that was barely making budget and not paying their pastor, this was an enormous amount.

We planned to surprise Joel with $5,000 to help his fundraising efforts. Though our cash flow was waning, we wanted to do something. I invited him to come to my church to preach on Father's Day. The real goal was to bring him up to Columbus to pamper him and then bless him.

After Joel finished preaching at the 9:30 am Experience, I surprised him on stage with a check for $2,500. He cried and the church stood and cheered with approval. What transpired next was one of the most incredible chain reactions of generosity I've ever seen.

I was standing in the lobby next to Joel when a lady walked up, extended her arm, and gave him the old *pentecostal handshake* (when someone slips you cash while shaking your hand so know else sees). Joel slid his hand in his pocket trying to be smooth.

"I think that woman just gave me some money," he leaned over and whispered.

I laughed and said, "Have you never had one of those handshakes?"

I got pulled in other directions by members of our church who wanted to connect. While I was distracted, people were approaching Joel with checks and cash. One gentleman drove home and came back with a thick envelope filled with about $1,500 in cash.

"Here, I won't do anything good with this," he said and handed Joel the envelope.

By the time I caught up with Joel in my Green Room, he was dumbfounded. Checks and cash were strewn across the table. He had a look of bewilderment on his face. He received an additional $4,000 in just a few minutes due to the generosity of the people in our church. The crazy thing is neither Joel nor I asked anyone to give.

I've never been prouder of my church.

The irony is we were in a message series about the early New Testament Church from the book of Acts. Joel was specifically preaching from this passage in Acts 4.

> There were no needy people among them,
> because those who owned land or houses
> would sell them and bring the money to the
> apostles to give to those in need.
>
> [Acts 4:34-35 NLT]

We were witnessing an Acts-like moment 2,000 years later.

Right before our 11:15 am Experience began, I bumped into Tony. He often seeks me out to shake my hand and tell me how blessed he is. Tony has a thin, wiry frame that's covered in tattoos from head to toe, literally. He's had a tough life, spending about 15 years in and out of prison. Though he never went to church, he decided to come with his girlfriend on Easter that year. God continued to draw him back. Just a couple weeks later, he surrendered his life to Jesus.

That morning, though, Tony looked dejected. I asked what was wrong and he told me how his car had recently been stolen and he didn't have any way to replace it. Even though he was struggling, he still believed he was blessed. I tried to encourage him in the short time we connected and then made my way into the auditorium.

As the next experience began, I received a text alert on my Apple watch from a young gentleman in our church. This guy was so moved by the message, he wanted to donate a car to the church so we could give it to someone in need. He and his wife recently bought a new vehicle and, for some reason, didn't want to trade in their old one. He figured they could sell it themselves for more than a dealership would offer. He works in finance and is always trying to operate in the most economical way. So, it was a *big* deal for him to want to give away a vehicle worth nearly $10,000. I thanked him for being obedient to God's prompting and then went back to singing like nothing just happened.

Then it hit me! I just had someone tell me he needs a car and less than ten minutes later someone else completely unaware wanted to donate their car to someone in need!

"This is God," I thought.

Yes, I was a little slow that morning.

I texted him back and asked permission to give the car away in this experience. He gave me the green light and even sent me a picture of it to put up on our LED screen.

After Joel's message, I surprised him with another check for $2,500. He lost it! Tears and snot freely flowing. He was experiencing his own miracle, and I was enjoying every moment of it. Then, what I can only describe as an Oprah moment, I called Tony up onto the platform and surprised him with a new vehicle in front of the entire church. The place erupted in praise! God gave our church a miraculous sermon illustration that day.

After the 11:15 am Experience, the same thing happened for Joel. People just kept giving him money. By the time Joel flew home on Monday, he had received over $25,000. And by the following weekend that total grew to more than $32,000. Besides the $5,000 the church gave to him, all of it was completely unplanned and unprovoked. It was a moment I will never forget.

There is something powerful about putting yourself in a position where God has to come through or you will fail! Joel and I both know that feeling. When we walk by faith, we are positioning ourselves to experience miracles like we witnessed that Father's Day weekend. And little did I know, that wasn't the only miracle coming.

"We need to draw $100,000 from our reserve account to pay our mortgage," Jenny, my Operations Manager texted me.

Eight days after our church generously blessed Joel, we didn't have enough in our accounts to pay the mortgage and staff. Our loan at *The Solomon Foundation* requires us to keep a three-month reserve in an account with them. We aren't supposed to touch those funds. But now we had to! We had only been in our new facility for nine months and already had to make the single largest withdrawal from our reserve account. The seriousness of our situation woke my soul up like someone dousing me with a bucket of cold water. We just upgraded to code Def Con Yellow. At this rate, we may be out of money by the end of the year.

Holding up your vision when it's leaking *provision* is like trying to plug leaks in Hoover Dam. It feels like it could implode at any point. I didn't know what to do, other than pray and freak out a little bit. This was the day I hoped would never arrive.

The next morning, I woke up, got ready, had my devotions, and then went to the gym per my typical routine. I was working my biceps when my phone buzzed with a new text message. It was from Penny, our bookkeeper. She sent me and Jenny a picture of what arrived in the mail that morning. A significant check. Can you guess how much for?

$100,000!

I couldn't believe it. I just stood there overwhelmed with emotion in the middle of the gym. I wanted to cry and shout at the same time. These kinds of things happen to *other* people. You know, the stories you've heard of people receiving a check for *exactly* what they needed in the 11th hour. All I could do was shake my head in disbelief and say, "Only God!"

Over the next two months, I continued negotiating the sale of the five acres. By September, we signed a contract to sell our parcel of land to a retail developer. Of course, I know that real estate contracts are never a sure bet. And yes, we are very much still in the *middle* of this contract as I write this. However, I can't help but wonder if God is once again bringing provision to us, even if it may take a year to see it.

That fall, we were continuing to pull from our reserves to support the ministry. By the end of November, Jenny dropped another bomb on us in our Executive Leadership Team meeting. She told us there was a good chance we'd be out of money by Spring of 2022. The room went quiet. We all just sat there stunned. In that moment, words weren't needed to express how we all felt. It just got real! We knew taking this big step of faith was scary, but hearing it said out loud was jolting.

We had been doing our best to eliminate all unnecessary expenses and even kept our Christmas expenses under budget. There wasn't much more we could do. I told the team I would email Doug at *The Solomon Foundation* and let him know our status. Our only hope of avoiding this disaster was a miracle — an end-of-year miracle.

For as long as I can remember, our church has taken up a year-end offering. It's the only time we ask our church to give to a special offering. We regularly talk about the importance of giving and stretching your faith in the area of finances without pushing it in people's faces. We don't even "pass the plate" during our Worship Experiences. This is the only time each year when I invite our church to participate in a free-will offering. We designate ten percent of what people give to the church for use through outreach, missions, or helping those struggling in our community. So, this is also an opportunity to join with our outreach partners to impact both our community and the world.

As we closed out 2021, we celebrated incredible stories of life change, baptized people every weekend, and prepared to give. Those special offering weekends are some of my favorites. I'm always moved by the hundreds of people who choose to give generously to what God is doing through their church.

But what God did at the end of that year is nothing short of a miracle in my eyes. We received more money than any previous end-of-year offerings, including when pre-pandemic attendance was higher. Our church gave more than $500,000 to help us continue doing ministry in 2022.

Can I say it again?

Only God!

Originally, I was not planning to write an epilogue. But in the past seven months, I have personally witnessed God's miraculous provision. I felt it was too important not to share with you how God was continuing to work in our situation. I understand an epilogue is supposed to tell you what happened *after* the story was over. But in our case, the story isn't over. We are still walking on the water, trusting God for His daily provision.

It always *encourages* my faith to hear that God is still working miracles. But it *builds* my faith to experience it firsthand. I hope our story encourages your faith. But I also pray you build *your faith* by stepping out and trusting God, regardless of how small it might seem. Faith is scary! But what is on the other side of that step of faith is the most thrilling adventure of your life.

So, what are you waiting for?

EPILOGUE

There has never been the slightest doubt in my mind that the God who started this great work in you would keep at it and bring it to a flourishing finish on the very day Christ Jesus appears.

[Philippians 1:6 MSG]

ACKNOWLEDGEMENTS

MY STORY IS NOT just the product of my hard work, but also the encouragement and support of friends, family, and a community that I love. I am blessed to have so many people in my corner following the crazy vision God has put within me. Without their faithful support, I would not have the courage to chase my God-given dreams. Without them, this book would not exist.

To my wife, Lorelei. Your quiet confidence is a bedrock for me. You work harder than anyone I know and possess a strength that can only come from above. You keep me grounded when my head gets in the clouds. And you've taught me how to see *people* when all I can see is a finish line. Thank you for being the most amazing mother to our wonderful girls, the glue for our family, and my co-pilot on this crazy journey. I could fail at everything else in life as long as I'm successful with you. I love you!

To my daughters, Lauryn and Audrey and son-in-law, Hunter. You have brought so much joy into my life. My greatest accomplishment is not the church I've built; it's the family I've raised. All of you reflect the heart and passion of Jesus. My greatest desire is to show you what it means to pursue God-sized dreams and use your life to build His Kingdom. Never let anyone limit what God can do through you.

To my parents, Paul and Myrna. I'm blessed to have two parents who love Jesus as much as both of you do. The reason I know and follow Jesus is because of the authentic example you set for me growing up. Your passion and love for Christ inspires me. Thank you for always praying for me and showing me what it looks like to live a life of prayer.

To Bob and Denise, my second parents. Not only did you allow me to marry your precious daughter, but you invited me into your family like I was your own. Words cannot express how grateful I am for your belief in me. Without you, our church would not exist. The pastor and leader I am today is because you stepped aside to allow an inexperienced and ambitious twenty-something-year-old lead. Your legacy carries on in our family and in our church.

To the incredible people at *The Solomon Foundation* and especially you, Russell. Thank you for believing in us and funding our vision. You do more than provide financial resources; you provide love and support to build God's Kingdom.

To my good friend and mentor, Tim. You have been a lifeline for me when I was drowning under the weight of this role. I still can't believe a mega-church pastor gave me his cell phone number the first time we met at a conference. God brought you into my life when I needed a mentor in ministry. Thank you for pouring into me.

To Matthew, Keith, and Konan, my co-laborers and friends in the ministry. Your wisdom and friendship over the years has helped me lead through the ups and downs. Keith, your leadership capital is always gold. Konan, your fire and passion for ministry is contagious. Matthew, you have been my best friend in ministry and in life. You are the most authentic leader I know. My respect for you goes beyond words.

To Jenny, Trae, and Russ, my Executive Leadership Team. You have helped shoulder the weight of leading our church and supported my crazy, faith-filled decisions. You are standing on the water with me. Jenny, thank you for the passion and skill you bring to running our church. Trae, thank you for the constant encouragement, kind words, and the many ways you support my creative ideas. Russ, thank you for bringing your heart and leadership to the team and all the suggested edits of this book. It's been a joy to be in this writing process with you.

To my staff. Thank you for allowing me to dream big and try new things. Your loyalty and support of the vision God has given me makes leading this church a dream. Your tireless effort and commitment to serve our church is the fuel for my faith. I wouldn't attempt what we have without it. A special thank you to Tucker, Hannah, Maria, and Christi for helping bring this book to life through your creative gifts.

To my X Church family. You have trusted me with your greatest treasure: your spiritual life. Your love and affection have made serving as your pastor one of the greatest honors of my life. I am humbled by the hundreds of families that have sacrificed and given to this audacious vision. I am forever grateful for our life-giving, imperfect, authentic, and inspiring community. Let's never settle for comfortable and continue to believe God for more. We will *Reach Thousands and Give Away Millions.*

Lastly, to those who have yet to hear and receive the gospel through our church. We took these risky, bold steps of faith for you. I am praying that one day, because of our faith and the grace of God, your eternity will forever be changed.

NOTES

Chapter 2: The Invitation

1. Best, Ashley Richards and Fuller, Amanda. "Real Science for Life: Buoyancy" Kentucky Teacher. Oct 27, 2016. https://www.kentuckyteacher.org/subjects/science/2016/10/real-science-for-real-life-buoyancy/

Chapter 4: God or Gut?

1. *The times. [volume]* (Richmond, Va.), 13 Jan. 1901. *Chronicling America: Historic American Newspapers.* Lib. of Congress. https://chroniclingamerica.loc.gov/lccn/sn85034438/1901-01-13/ed-1/seq-8/

2. Begdache, Lina. "Ask a Scientist: Neurons help explain how our brains think" Pressconnects. Mar 17, 2019. https://www.pressconnects.com/story/news/local/2019/03/18/ask-scientist-how-do-thoughts-work-our-brain/3153303002/

3. "How do we hear?" National Institute of Deafness and other Communication Disorders. May 2015. https://www.nidcd.nih.gov/health/how-do-we-hear

4. Roswandowitz, et al. "Obligatory and facultative brain regions for voice-identity recognition" Oxford Academic. Brain, Volume 141, Issue 1. January 2018. P 234-247. https://academic.oup.com/brain/article/141/1/234/4708308

5. "Humans Have Around 6,200 Thoughts in a Single Day, shows New Study" News 18. Jul 19, 2020. https://www.news18.com/news/buzz/humans-have-around-6200-thoughts-in-a-single-day-shows-new-study-2723281.html

Chapter 6: Opportunity Isn't Knocking

1. Martin, Emmie. "Apple just hit a $1 trillion market cap—here's why its little-known third co-founder sold his 10% stake for $800" CNBC. Aug 2, 2018
https://www.cnbc.com/2018/08/02/why-ronald-wayne-sold-his-10-percent-stake-in-apple-for-800-dollars.html

Chapter 7: Opposition Is Knocking

1. "About CDC's Work on Birth Defects" Centers for Disease Control and Prevention. Oct 28, 2020.
https://www.cdc.gov/ncbddd/birthdefects/aboutus.html

Chapter 8: When the Gap Gets Bigger

1. King, Bob. "9,096 Stars in the Sky—Is that all?" Sky & Telescope. Sep 27, 2014.
https://skyandtelescope.org/astronomy-blogs/how-many-stars-night-sky-09172014/

2. "Dark Energy, Dark Matter" NASA.gov
https://science.nasa.gov/astrophysics/focus-areas/what-is-dark-energy

Chapter 10: The Anatomy of Fear & Faith

1. "Trivia About Kings Island" (Press release). Kings Island/Cedar Fair. 2008.

2. "The Limbic System" The University of Queensland.
https://qbi.uq.edu.au/brain/brain-anatomy/limbic-system

3. Bancos M.D., Irina "Adrenal Hormones" Endocrine Society. Last Updated: Jan 23, 2022
https://www.endocrine.org/patient-engagement/endocrine-library/hormones-and-endocrine-function/adrenal-hormones

4. "How can DHEA benefit your Health?" Medical News Today. https://www.endocrine.org/patient-engagement/endocrine-library/hormones-and-endocrine-function/adrenal-hormones

5. Sripada, et al. "DHEA Enhances Emotion Regulation Neurocircuits and Modulates Memory for Emotional Stimuli" Neuropsychopharmacology, Issue 38. 1798-1807. Apr 3, 2013. https://www.nature.com/articles/npp201379

6. Lavin, et al "The anterior cingulate cortex: an integrative hub for human socially-driven interactions" Frontiers in Neuroscience. May 8, 2013. https://www.frontiersin.org/articles/10.3389/fnins.2013.00064/full

7. Thayer and Smith. Greek Lexicon entry for Sophron. The KJV New Testament Greek Lexicon. https://www.biblestudytools.com/lexicons/greek/kjv/sophron.html

8. "The Power of Positive Thinking" John Hopkins Medicine. https://www.hopkinsmedicine.org/health/wellness-and-prevention/the-power-of-positive-thinking

9. McGonigal, Ph.D, Kelly "The Upside of Stress: why stress is good for you and how to get good at it" New York: Penguin Random House, May 10, 2016. (Kindle) p. 16

Chapter 11: Embrace the Mystery

1. "George Land, Ph.D. (1932-2016)" World Business Academy. https://worldbusiness.org/fellows/george-land-ph-d/

2. Vint, Larry "Fresh Thinking Drives Creativity & Innovation" Journal of the Queensland Society for Information Technology in Education, 2005. https://research-repository.griffith.edu.au/bitstream/handle/10072/7880/33187_1.pdf

MEET THE AUTHOR

Tim and his wife, Lorelei, have been married since 1996. They currently reside in the Columbus, Ohio area along with their two daughters, Audrey and Lauryn with her husband Hunter.

 Tim is the founding and lead pastor of X Church. His passion in ministry is preaching, reaching those far from Christ, and helping people fall in love with the Scriptures. He also co-hosts a weekly podcast helping people learn to think like Jesus in a counter-cultural world.

Tim enjoys listening to books, having deep intellectual conversations about science and theology, working out, golfing, playing drums, creating music, and competitive shooting.

Tim would love to hear how God used this book to prompt your heart to move in *Scary Faith*. Share your story through email at *stories@scaryfaithbook.com*.

If you are interested in more content or would like Tim to speak at your church, conference, school, or event, visit his website: *www.timmoore.online*.

HEY! LET'S CONNECT!

TIM MOORE

⊙ @PASTORTIMMOORE

f @PASTORTIMMOORE

🐦 @PASTORTIMMOORE

WWW.TIMMOORE.ONLINE